10

MINUTE GUIDE TO

MOTIVATING PEOPLE

by Marshall J. Cook

alpha books

Macmillan Spectrum/Alpha Books

A Division of Macmillan General Reference
A Simon and Schuster Macmillan Company
1633 Broadway, New York, NY 10019

International Standard Book Number: 0-02-861738-x
Library of Congress Catalog Card Number: 97-071164

99 98 97   8 7 6 5 4 3 2 1

Interpretation of the printing code: the rightmost double-digit number is the year of the book's first printing; the rightmost single-digit number is the number of the book's printing. For example, a printing code of 97-1 shows that this copy of the book was printed during the first printing of the book in 1997.

Printed in the United States of America

Note: Reasonable care has been taken in the preparation of the text to ensure its clarity and accuracy. This book is sold with the understanding that the author and the publisher are not engaged in rendering legal, accounting, or other professional service. Laws vary from state to state, and readers with specific financial questions should seek the services of a professional advisor.

The author and publisher specifically disclaim any liability, loss, or risk, personal or otherwise, which is incurred as a consequence, directly or indirectly, of the use and application of any of the contents of this book.

This is a *CWL Publishing Enterprises Book*, developed by John A. Woods for Macmillan Spectrum/Alpha Books. For more information, contact CWL Publishing Enterprises, 3010 Irvington Way, Madison, WI 53713-3414, (608) 273-3710.

Publisher: Theresa Murtha
Editor in Chief: Richard J. Staron
Production Editor: Michael Thomas
Copy Editor: Mike McFeely
Cover Designer: Dan Armstrong
Designer: Glenn Larsen
Indexer: Eric Brinkman
Production Team: Angela Calvert, Christy Wagner, Maureen West

CONTENTS

1 CHANNEL MOTIVATION FOR PEAK PERFORMANCE — 1

Motivation and Peak Performance 1

What We Really Want Out of Work 3

Five Ways to Achieve Peak Performance by Making Sure Your Coworkers Feel Respected in the Workplace 4

Five Ways to Help Your Coworkers Participate in Decision-Making 5

Five Ways to Get Your Coworkers Working Together, *with* You Rather Than *for* You 5

2 LEAD FOR COMMITMENT, DON'T MANAGE FOR COMPLIANCE — 7

Every Team Needs a Leader 7

The Difference Between a Boss and a Leader 9

Obedient Workers Aren't Motivated Workers 11

Commitment, Not Compliance 12

3 IT ALL STARTS WITH A VISION—YOURS — 15

The Importance of a Vision 16

Three Things a Vision *Isn't* 17

Four Qualities of a Powerful Vision 19

4 TALKING YOUR TALK — 20

Using Word Pictures to Communicate and Motivate 20

Make Sure Your Word Pictures Fit the Situation 23

Plain Talk 23

5 Meetings that Motivate   28

The Value of Meetings 28
Conducting Effective Meetings 30

**6 Turn Every Employee Into a Creative
    (and Motivated) Problem Solver   38**

Let Your Employees Solve Their (and Your) Problems 38
Brainstorming 40
The Tale of the Student and the Barometer 42

7 When Work Is Its Own Reward   45

The Parable of the Pop Machine 46
Something That Doesn't Reinforce Good Performance 51

8 Reward What You Want   52

Rewards and Motivation to Perform 52
What Makes the Most Effective Reward? 54

9 Coaching and Motivation   59

A Coaching Example 59
Some Lessons in Coaching 62
Why You Shouldn't Name an "Employee of the Month" 64
Creating Winners 64

**10 Correcting Mistakes Without
    Destroying Motivation   66**

Mistakes: They Happen 66
The Case for Saying Nothing 67
Some Ways to Help Employees When They
    Make Mistakes 70

11 Time Management for Motivation   74

Are You Busy or Are You Productive? 74

First Principle of Time Management for Motivation 75

Second Principle of Time Management for Motivation 76

Third Principle of Time Management for Motivation 77

Fourth Principle of Time Management for Motivation 78

Fifth Principle of Time Management for Motivation 80

Sixth Principle of Time Management for Motivation 81

Seventh Principle of Time Management for Motivation 81

What Do You Do With All the Time You Save? 82

**12 Reducing Stress and Enhancing
     Motivation   83**

Stress and Performance 83

Why Lack of Stress Isn't the Answer to the
   Stress Problem 85

Stop Her! She's on a Roll! 87

The Plight of the Adrenaline Junkie 87

Taking a Vacation—Several Times a Day 88

Three More Ways You Can Help Your Coworkers
   Get Unstressed 91

**13 Don't Just Train the Worker—
     Educate the Person   94**

Training as a Chance to Get Better, Not as an
   Indicator of Poor Performance 95

Finding the Right Training 96

Don't Overlook Special Training Needs and
   Opportunities 98

Let the Trainee Become the Trainer 98

Sometimes Training Becomes Something More—
an Education 99

Basic Training: Sharing the Big Picture 100

14 If You Want to Keep Them Motivated, You've Got to Earn Their Trust   101

Trust, Leadership, and Motivation 101

The Truth, the Same Truth, and Nothing But the Truth 102

Match Your Actions to Your Words 104

Four Reasons Why We Don't Tell Them Enough 104

Invite and Pay Attention to Disagreement and Criticism ... 105

Don't Get Caught in a Triangle 106

Admit Your Mistakes 107

15 Trust Has to Go Both Ways   109

Why You Can't Lead Them If You Don't Trust Them 109

Don't They Have to Earn Your Trust? 110

A Way to Show You Trust Your Coworkers: Respect Their
Privacy 111

16 How to Avoid Being the (Worst) Boss of the Year   117

Scrooge and Motivation 117

Meet Real-Life, Modern-Day Scrooges 118

Drum Roll, Please, for the Worst Bosses of the Year—
or Any Year 119

Does *Dilbert* Make You Laugh—or Wince? 120

What Scrooge Can Teach Us 121

17 WHAT DO WORKERS *REALLY* WANT, ANYWAY? **123**

The Way Things Really Are 123

What We Want From Work 124

And What You Can Do About It 125

INDEX **129**

INTRODUCTION

Motivation is a tricky subject. There's always some question about whether one person can motivate another. The premise of this book is that you *can't* motivate another person. Motivation comes from within. However, you *can* affect what a person might be motivated to do. And how you affect the motivation of others to perform well is what this book is all about.

A good manager and leader understands that people are always motivated to do what they believe to be in their best interests. Employees who seem to have outstanding motivation on the job have somehow come to believe that working hard and doing a good job for the organization is in their best interests. They identify their welfare with that of the organization.

The question becomes how can a manager create a situation at work that helps an employee come to equate their personal welfare with doing a good job? In other words, how does one positively affect motivation on the job? The answers to these questions is what this book is all about.

Briefly, it involves cultivating a mutually supportive relationship with employees. Managers who focus on doing this in every job situation will soon have a whole group of motivated employees on their hands. And at the same time they will find their level of motivation raised as well.

Does this sound like a promising proposition? Then read these 10-minute lessons to find out more.

CONVENTIONS USED IN THIS BOOK

This book uses three types of icons to help you quickly find important information:

 Timesaver Tip icons offer ideas that cut corners and avoid confusion.

 Plain English icons define new terms.

 Panic Button icons identify potential problem areas and how to solve them.

ACKNOWLEDGMENTS

This book came to be because of two people: Dick Staron and John Woods. Dick, editor-in-chief at Macmillan General Reference, commissioned John Woods of CWL Publishing Enterprises to develop this book. John asked me to write it and then supported me throughout the process. I want to thank both of them. And thank you for selecting this book to help learn about how to positively affect the motivation of the people you work with and your own motivation at the same time.

THE AUTHOR

Marshall J. Cook is professor of journalism in the division of continuing studies at the University of Wisconsin, Madison. He teaches seminars, workshops, and credit courses on writing, time management, media relations, and other business-related subjects. He is a contributor to magazines such as *Business Age* and *World Executive Digest*. He is the author of *Slow Down— And Get More Done*, a book on time management. He has been a frequent guest on television and radio shows to discuss this and various other business- and management-related subjects. He publishes his own newsletter on writing and related issues called *Creativity Connection*.

1

Channel Motivation for Peak Performance

In this lesson you'll learn that you don't actually motivate people.
You provide direction for the motivation they already have.

Motivation and Peak Performance

Whether you're a new supervisor or a veteran, whether you
have a background in management or worked your way up
through the ranks, you need to know something important
about motivating peak performance from the people you
work with.

You can't do it.

Not with criticism or praise, reward or punishment, carrots or
sticks.

Nothing you do will motivate anyone to do anything. They're
already motivated. Don't waste time trying to give them what
they've already got.

Motivation An inner drive, impulse, or intention that causes a person to act in a certain way or to achieve a certain goal.

You want to see that motivation? Check out your employees at quitting time. Watch them playing softball. Get them talking about their kids. You'll hardly ever find an unmotivated worker after hours.

It Comes From Within Motivation comes from inside, not outside. You don't motivate. You draw on and provide direction for the motivation that's already there.

What motivates the people who work with you? The same things that motivate you. We all need food, shelter, and clothing, and we'll work to get them. We want good benefits—especially health care. We want the chance to earn raises and advancements. We want job security.

Give Them What You Can Even if you can't do much about wages and benefits, you can communicate performance standards clearly, consistently, and honestly and give employees the freedom to do the job in the best way they know how, so folks have a chance to earn the things they want and need.

Wages and benefits aren't the only reasons we work. In fact, sometimes the money doesn't have much to do with why we're working at one job instead of another or at one company instead of another. We brings lots of other motivations to the workplace.

WHAT WE REALLY WANT OUT OF WORK

When do you feel the best about yourself on the job? No matter what you're doing and who you're doing it for, I'll bet you feel the best when you feel committed to the task. You believe in what you're doing. You believe you're doing some good for somebody as well as for yourself.

I'll bet you also feel a sense of freedom and mastery. You make choices, and you perform your tasks effectively.

I've felt this commitment, freedom, and mastery while teaching a class in remedial reading. I've also felt it resealing my driveway. I've felt it coaching Little League baseball.

What do we want—besides the money—from going to work?

- We want a chance to do good work.
- We want our work to make a difference.
- We want to make a contribution.
- We want to learn and master new skills.

Idealistic? You bet. Unrealistic? I don't think so. You feel these motivations, and so do the people who work with you.

We feel that we have basic rights in the workplace:

- The right to some control over our actions
- The right to be respected, trusted, and supported
- The right to be treated fairly
- The right to have our effort recognized and our good work rewarded

We also have basic requirements to enable us to do good work:

- Proper equipment and sufficient materials
- A chance to define problems and create solutions
- A voice in the decisions that affect us
- Appropriate training and updating

If you're a manager and want to get the most from your co-workers, you have to make sure that they get these things. Do that and you'll have productive workers—and a happy manager. Do the job for your workers, and you do the job for your employer. You win when they win.

 tip **Defining Your Role**   Your primary responsibility to the people who pay your salary is to help your coworkers do their work well.

What, specifically, can you do to help your coworkers?

FIVE WAYS TO ACHIEVE PEAK PERFORMANCE BY MAKING SURE YOUR COWORKERS FEEL RESPECTED IN THE WORKPLACE

1. Don't just manage. *Coach* for peak performance.
2. Explain how their work fits in with and contributes to larger goals.
3. Coordinate their separate efforts for that larger goal.
4. Encourage and nurture learning, growth, mastery, and independence.
5. Give honest, timely feedback on performance.

FIVE WAYS TO HELP YOUR COWORKERS PARTICIPATE IN DECISION-MAKING

1. Communicate your goals and expectations clearly.

2. Discuss every decision that affects their work.

3. Listen.

4. Seek consensus.

5. Provide full access to information.

FIVE WAYS TO GET YOUR COWORKERS WORKING TOGETHER, *WITH* YOU RATHER THAN *FOR* YOU

1. Foster an atmosphere in which people can enjoy their work and each other.

2. Advocate for them and their needs to upper management.

3. Fight for them when necessary.

4. Create group as well as individual goals.

5. Reward cooperation.

In short, you can create a work environment in which the people who work with you can claim and use their talents and abilities to the fullest—just as you'll be able to claim and use yours.

Create a Positive Environment   You can't *not* create environment. By your words and even more by your actions, you'll tell your workers what you think of them, what you expect of them, and what kind of working relationships you want to have with them. So remember to ask yourself, "What kind of environment am I creating?" Make sure your answer is one that promotes rather than hinders motivation and performance.

You create environment by accident if you don't do it on purpose. They'll give back what they get. They'll mirror your attitudes and your behavior because you're teaching them the way to get ahead in the organization. (After all, your behavior got you where you are, right?) Not much of this will take place on a conscious level, but it's quite real, shaping attitudes and directing actions.

They'll Do As You Do, Not As You Say   If your words say one thing, but your actions say another, they'll believe your actions.

You've got to walk your talk. "My door is always open," you assure them. But in fact your door is closed most of the time. Or it's open, but you're not in your office. Or you're there but not available. Or you meet with them but don't really listen to what they say.

What do they believe, what you say or what you do? Actions really do speak louder than words every time.

In this lesson you learned that you don't actually motivate people. You provide direction for the motivation they already have. The rest of the lessons in this book deal with how you'll use your words and your actions to do that important job.

2

LEAD FOR COMMITMENT, DON'T MANAGE FOR COMPLIANCE

In this lesson you'll learn to see your job as that of a leader seeking commitment to common goals, not as a boss seeking compliance to orders.

EVERY TEAM NEEDS A LEADER

We've run through a lot of management theories in recent years.

We've created quality circles, preached intrapreneuring, formed strategic alliances.

We've tried management by wandering around and management by objectives.

We've developed synergy and shifted paradigms.

Through all of these changing theories, workers have wanted and needed the same things they've always wanted and needed—good work to do and appreciation for doing it.

Going with the Flow No matter what the current trendy management philosophy is, workers figure out how to adapt to it and hold on to their jobs. Recognize and use this to plug into their motivation to achieve excellence.

Workers don't need you to try to shift their paradigms. Here's what they *do* need, however:

- They need you to tell them what they're expected to do and how well they're doing it.
- They need you to show them where their effort fits into the overall picture.
- They need you to provide the tools and training they need to do their jobs well.
- They need you to advocate and fight for them with upper management when they're not getting what they need.
- They need you to help solve problems, making sure you don't solve the wrong problem or create a new problem—or *become* the problem.
- They need you to help them improve and get better.

To be an effective manager, you need to do all these things. And when you do them you'll start to be not just a manager, but a leader.

The manager of a baseball team decides who plays and who sits on the bench, he makes out the lineup, and he determines strategy. Then it's up to the players to make the plays and carry out the strategy.

A good team also needs a leader. By word and by example, a leader gets the most from the other members of the team, influencing, guiding, inspiring—all of which affects their motivation in positive ways. A leader is every bit as important to the success of a team as the manager—maybe more so. You should be the leader of your team.

 You Either Lead or You Don't You can't be a bad leader. You're either a leader or you're not. And leaders bring out the best in people, period.

- Leaders don't push, they pull. That means you have to be out in front.
- Leaders don't coerce, they persuade. That means you have to talk with, not just to, your teammates.
- The leader wins or loses with the team. The success of the leader is tied to the success of the team.

 Only One Path to Leadership You can't declare yourself leader. You become the leader the moment your workers decide to follow you. There's no other way to do it. And they only follow you when they believe you have their best interests in mind.

Your authority doesn't come from the job title. It comes from the people you work with. They decide to follow you because they want to go in the same direction you're going, and you seem to know how to get there.

THE DIFFERENCE BETWEEN A BOSS AND A LEADER

The leader coaches, teaches, demonstrates, urges, coaxes—does anything and everything necessary to help the others perform up to and sometimes even beyond their capacities.

The coach explains the goal and the steps needed to reach that goal. Effective coaches don't just talk it; they demonstrate, correct, encourage, and exhort every step of the way. Then they stay on the sideline and let the players play the game.

Here's the difference between the old-style boss and the manager-leader:

THE BOSS	THE LEADER
Talks	Listens
Keeps control	Shares control
Gives directions	Asks questions
Fixes mistakes	Coaches
Judges after	Helps throughout
Takes credit	Gives credit
Finds weaknesses	Builds on strengths
Fosters dependence	Demands independence
Punishes failure	Rewards effort and risk
Reprimands in public	Praises in public
Praises in private—if ever	Guides in private

Seeking Commitment   Bosses demand obedience and compliance. Leaders develop commitment. Commitment comes from employees believing the leader views his or her role as helping them to succeed. And this is a major contributor to an individual's motivation to perform at a high level.

Being a leader is a tall order. But leadership actually takes less time and energy than being a boss—while boosting productivity and morale. Imagine the difference in your motivation working *for* a boss compared to working *with* a leader.

OBEDIENT WORKERS AREN'T MOTIVATED WORKERS

Obedient workers perform diligently—as long as the boss is watching. They do what's necessary to escape punishment (reprimand, pay cut, suspension, demotion, termination) and earn reward (praise, raise, advancement).

But what happens when you're not looking? Not much.

Obedient workers put in the minimum necessary to get by. They won't take initiative, won't offer solutions to problems, won't take risks. Why should they?

> **!** **Excellence, Not Compliance**   When you demand compliance, you get compliance—and nothing more. Compliance does not breed excellence. At best it results in average performance and at worst it's a formula for mediocrity.

Underneath that compliance, your loyal employee may be seething with resentment, just waiting for a chance to undermine you.

> **Compliance** Giving in to a request, wish, or demand whether a person believes in it or not.

COMMITMENT, NOT COMPLIANCE

You don't want compliant subordinates. You want committed coworkers, who identify their self-interest with yours and with excellent job performance. They'll work just as hard and just as well when you're not watching—because they're not working *for* you, they're working *with* you.

Commitment   A pledge or promise, freely given. It suggests personal identification with a goal or an organization that motivates one to take actions to achieve that goal or contribute to the success of the organization.

We've all had supervisors who treated the people they worked with as if they were lazy and untrustworthy. These pit bosses nagged, checked up, bribed, and threatened. They encouraged gossip and gathered scraps of "evidence" to use against their workers, all in the name of "keeping them in line."

Does that sort of treatment motivate you? Sure. It motivates you to do as little as you can get away with, put in your time, go through the motions, grab your paycheck, and clear out.

Supervisors of this sort aren't trying to help people feel motivated. They're trying to *control*, through fear and greed. They bring out the worst in their work force.

Lead, Don't Control   You don't want to control "subordinates." You want to lead coworkers. Subordinates require superiors. Coworkers require commitment and effort to achieve shared goals— which leaders inspire.

Subordinate   Someone who is inferior to or below another in rank, power, or importance in an organization.

Insubordination   Disobedience or rebellion. It comes from people feeling that they have been treated unjustly.

Avoid Insubordination   If you put people in a subordinate position, you invite insubordination. Treat them with respect, as equals, and you earn cooperation.

You don't give up your authority when you treat workers as equals and seek their commitment. You're still in charge. You can't evade your responsibilities as a manager even if you want to. You must provide vision and direction. You must turn that vision into specific goals and lay out the plan for achieving those goals. You must communicate honestly and clearly, letting coworkers know what you expect from them and what they can expect from you.

When you do, you enhance your real authority.

It's the difference between a contract and a compact. You can enforce a contract, if you have to, by taking the other guy to court—an ugly mess at best. You never have to enforce a compact, because you build a compact on shared expectations and goals and on mutual respect and trust.

Compact A compact is a moral understanding between people that sets up expectations for how they will treat one another. People enter into a compact with others with whom they share values and goals.

Here's how the compact works:

WHAT A WORKER CAN EXPECT	WHAT A LEADER CAN EXPECT
A fair wage	An honest day's work
The right to learn	The responsibility to know
The right to help decide	The responsibility to participate in decision-making
Fairness	Fairness
Consistency	Consistency
Honesty	Honesty

You can't create this sort of compact with words alone. You have to live up to your part of the bargain. And when you do, you automatically trigger the motivation to perform at the same time.

In this lesson you learned to see your job as being a *leader*, seeking commitment to common goals, and not as a *boss*, seeking compliance to orders.

3

IT ALL STARTS WITH A VISION— YOURS

In this lesson you'll learn why you need to develop a clear vision that will help motivate you and your coworkers.

I recently helped conduct a forum with a group of nervous, resentful workers. The company was losing a major funding source (35 percent of its operating budget) and in response was reorganizing, which in this case meant merging four units into two.

Nobody was using words like "layoff" or "reduction in force," but management was getting a lot of mileage out of "attrition" and could guarantee only that a "significant core force" of workers would be retained under the new structure.

Folks were worried—and rightly so—that they would either lose their jobs or be asked to take on more work for less pay.

Three members of the management team held an open session to field employee questions, trying to boost morale while drumming up support for the reorganization plan.

Most of the questions boiled down to the basics: Will I still have a job when the dust settles? If so, will it look anything like the job I have now?

One question stood out. A part-time employee in a relatively vulnerable unit asked, "Can you tell us exactly why you're doing this reorganization? What do you hope to accomplish?"

Before the managers could respond, she added, "And don't just talk about money. That isn't enough."

She didn't use the word, but she was asking for a vision.

Vision   Describes the way things should be. If everything were just exactly as it ought to be, what would it look like? That's your vision.

You Need Vision   Yes, you want to stay in business. Yes, you want to make a profit. But that isn't reason enough for a worker who is being asked to work and sacrifice for the common good.

THE IMPORTANCE OF A VISION

The managers didn't have or couldn't define a vision that day. Instead, they talked about "increased efficiencies" and "new synergies," vague non-answers that left every employee just as unsettled as when they came in. Worse, it left them with the sense that nobody knew where the organization was headed.

You Need Direction   Baseball manager and malapropism expert Casey Stengel once said, "If you don't know where you're going, you might end up somewhere else." If you don't have a vision, get one. It helps you know where you're going.

Stengel knew where he was going, managing the New York Yankees to ten American League pennants and seven World Series titles.

Casey had a vision, a sense of how the game ought to be played. Up until then, teams played the same eight players day in and day out, substituting only in case of serious injury. But Casey thought every person on the team ought to contribute. His system for rotating players for peak performance came to be known as "platooning," and it's standard practice today.

Like Casey, you need a vision, a clear grasp of where your organization ought to be going, what it ought to look like on the way, and what it is going to look like when it gets there.

 It Doesn't Take an Expert   You don't have to be a visionary to have a vision. You just have to think about what you want to do and why you want to do it.

What President Bush used to call "the vision thing" isn't really all that mysterious.

Three Things a Vision *Isn't*

1. *A vision isn't a mission statement.*

Your organization may already have a mission statement. If so, I'll bet most of your coworkers can't tell you what it is. They also don't care. "Mission statement" sounds about as exciting as "tax return" and every bit as fun to prepare.

Whether you've got one or not, a mission statement isn't the same as a vision. Your mission statement names the game you're playing and your desire to play it successfully. It can often be summed up in a single sentence:

"We intend to become the number one supplier of top-quality dry cell batteries in the Midwest."

Mission statements state goals. They're important. But they aren't visions.

2. *A vision isn't a slogan.*

Lots of organizations use terms such as "premier," "dominant," and "top-quality" to describe themselves. There's nothing wrong with wanting to be the best. But don't mistake a bumper-sticker pep talk for a real vision.

3. *A vision isn't a policy manual.*

Every organization needs policies and procedures—specific guidelines for day-to-day operations and methods for resolving conflicts. But these policies and procedures aren't a vision to guide your organization, any more than the motor vehicle code provides a vision for handling the increase in traffic on a stressed highway system.

So, if a vision isn't a mission statement, a bumper sticker, or a policy manual, just what is it?

Here's an example of a vision, the "aspiration statement" for Levi Strauss & Co., the folks who make all those pants:

"We all want a company that our people are proud of and committed to, where all employees have an opportunity to contribute, learn, grow and advance based on merit....We want all our people to feel respected, treated fairly, listened to and involved. Above all, we want satisfaction from accomplishment and friendships...and to have fun in our endeavors."

I especially like this vision statement because it focuses on the employee's well-being. It deals with concepts such as respect, growth, and fairness, and it dares to suggest that we should be having fun at work. To me, that's a vision worth working to realize. It's a vision designed to make employees feel motivated to perform well.

 Being General Is Okay Don't get bogged down in particulars. First you need to know where you want to go. Then you can get out the maps and start figuring out how to get there.

FOUR QUALITIES OF A POWERFUL VISION

A vision is:

- A portrait of greatness, how things ought to be
- An expression of your highest hope
- The product of your heart and your gut as well as your head
- Values-based

A vision describes not just where you want to be and what you want to be like, but why you want to be there and what contribution you'll be making, what purpose you'll be serving, beyond making a profit.

Your vision should excite and inspire you. If it doesn't, it isn't much of a vision. And if it doesn't, then you certainly can't expect it to excite, inspire, or motivate anybody else.

In this lesson you learned why you need to develop a clear vision that will help motivate you and your coworkers.

4

TALKING YOUR TALK

In this lesson you'll learn how to use language that gets your message across clearly and helps your coworkers feel more motivated to work with you.

You can't turn your vision into reality by yourself. You'll need to bring your coworkers along with you—every last one of them.

You'll need to create a sense of shared meaning, a common interpretation of reality. Only then will you achieve coordinated action.

Huh?

I said, unless everybody rows in the same direction, the boat won't move forward.

Ah. Why didn't you just say so?

The point is: How you can expect people to feel motivated to work with you if they don't understand what you have on your mind?

USING WORD PICTURES TO COMMUNICATE AND MOTIVATE

Your workplace isn't a boat; it's an office building or a factory floor or a national forest. And your "crew" doesn't row. They staple, collate, weld, word process, sweep, paint, program, or put out fires. I used the word picture of the boat to clarify my vague, fuzzy language about "shared meaning" and "common interpretation."

Word Picture A word picture means using concrete words to evoke images that help people understand an idea. "The path is steep and rocky, but we have good hiking boots" is a word picture for "This project is going to be difficult, but we can do it."

Picture Perfect Use words to make pictures. This makes your message concrete and easy to understand. In other words, when communicating, try to be concrete, not abstract.

Here's another example, from Jeff MacNelly's comic strip, *Shoe*.

"We're taking this disagreement to alternative dispute resolution," the boss tells the employee—who of course doesn't know what the boss is talking about.

"It's when you get two alternatives to settle up the dispute," the boss explains, "my way or the highway."

That we can understand. We may not like it, but we understand it.

Keep It Simple Use clear, simple language. Don't use long words when short ones will work just as well and be more understandable.

My high school physics teacher, Mr. Stanton, was great at using word pictures to help us understand abstract concepts. He explained jet propulsion, for example, by asking us to remember what happens when you blow up a balloon and let it go. We could all see that balloon flying around the room. A lot of air rushing to get through a small hole makes a mighty push in the opposite direction—in a balloon or a jet engine.

To illustrate the law of thermodynamics that says "For every action there's an equal and opposite reaction," Stanton asked us to imagine what would happen if we tried to step from a rowboat onto a dock without having somebody hold the rowboat steady.

Splash. We got it.

I remember Stanton's word pictures—and the concepts behind them—to this day. And I felt more motivated to study and learn physics because I understood it.

Former presidents Ronald Reagan and Jimmy Carter are good examples of the use and non-use of word pictures. Reagan, "The Great Communicator," told stories. Carter cited statistics and spoke in generalities. Reagan communicated his vision of "morning in America," and it motivated a lot of people to vote for him. Carter was whipped badly in his bid for a second term and will probably be remembered as a fine, intelligent man who couldn't inspire or move people.

Make Sure It's Clear   Word pictures are great, but remember that the picture must be appropriate to the subject and the audience. Otherwise, it's just another unclear statement that won't help you get people on your side.

MAKE SURE YOUR WORD PICTURES FIT THE SITUATION

In business, traditionally a male-dominated bastion, we've used the language of war to describe the way we do business. We rally the troops and send them well-armed to do battle in the trenches. Or the war moves from the battlefield to the football field, which we insist must be level, where we go for the long bomb, try an end run, or blitz the opposition.

Effective? Probably not. We've used the same language so long and so often, it no longer creates a picture. It's a cliché.

Appropriate? That's doubtful, too. Despite what some of the textbooks tell you, business *isn't* a war, or even a football game, and images of violent competition and combat may not properly represent your vision of how you should be conducting your business. Do you really want to think of the competition as an enemy to be wiped out?

Ready to talk your talk in pictures? Sure you are. You do it all the time. If you say you saw the "sun rise," for example, you're using picture language, since the sun doesn't really "rise."

You don't have to be profound. You don't have to sound important. You just have to be clear and sincere.

PLAIN TALK

Plain talk is the best talk. Bill Rivers, my college journalism mentor, advocated what he called the "plain style" of writing, "language in its shirt sleeves." He hated pompous, inflated language, always seeking instead the most simple, clear, and direct way to communicate. "Have the courage to write simply," he told us often.

"Simply" I understood, or thought I did, anyway. But "courage"? Why was plain talk a matter of bravery?

Like most guidelines worth hanging onto, I had to grow into this one. I had to get out into the world and find out the hard way that communicating in plain, simple words really does take guts. If people understand what you're saying, they might not like it—or you.

That probably explains why some folks retreat into overblown nonsense like the following mess, taken from a memo from a school district supervisor:

"It is necessary that schools and school districts emphasize the importance of imparting to students the skills and attitudes which are the underpinnings of a comfortable, confident, successful producer of all forms of written matter."

Say what?

This guy must be really smart and really important to use so many big words, right? Wrong. He wants to *seem* smart and important. Or maybe he doesn't really want us to understand what he's saying. Or maybe he doesn't understand what he's talking about. In any case, such a statement isn't likely to make us feel motivated to help out.

When you boil all that blather down, doesn't it just mean, "Schools should teach students how to write"? So, why didn't he just say so?

For the same reason all those tubes of toothpaste assure us that the goop inside the tube is "an effective decay preventative dentifrice when used in a conscientiously applied program of oral hygiene and regular professional care." Meaning: If you brush your teeth and go to the dentist, this stuff might help keep you from getting cavities.

It that *all*? That's all.

Clear Is Best   Whatever you want to say, say it as clearly and directly as possible. If you find that hard, it's probably because you aren't sure what you want to say. Don't say it until you *are* sure. And if you aren't sure, you can be sure that your listeners won't be, either.

DON'T BE PASSIVE IN YOUR COMMUNICATION

Along with big words and endless sentences, you also want to avoid the passive voice. Be active with your communication.

Passive Voice   Backward language. Passive voice: "The ball got passed by John Elway." Active voice: "John Elway passed the ball."

Consider the following:

"It has been decided that all breaks must be taken in increments of no more than seven minutes' duration."

Inflated words are part of the problem. What's a break that must be taken "in increments of no more than seven minutes' duration"? A seven-minute break. Right?

It's also passive ("It *has been decided* that all breaks *must be taken...*"). We don't know for sure who's taking the breaks, and we don't know who's deciding how long those breaks have to be. Passive voice is unclear and evasive. It's another type of communication that can confuse and put people off. And it undermines their motivation to work with you.

Be Plain and Simple   Say it straight. Take responsibility for your decisions. Use plain, simple words in the active voice. Save the manure for the garden.

AVOID EUPHEMISMS

We've created all sorts of inventive ways to say we're going to fire people. We downsize, dehire, decruit, deselect, and a load of other "de-" words. We enroll you in the "Golden Years Program" (early retirement with loss of benefits) and subject you to a "Career Progression Review" (CPR), in which you "progress" to job termination.

It's not enough to get fired. You have to have your intelligence insulted on your way out the door.

This is a pusillanimous behavior pattern.

Huh?

It's cowardly to hide behind big words.

Be clear. Be direct. Be specific.

"You need to improve your telephone answering skills," the manager says to the employee.

"Fine," says the employee. "No problem. I'll get right on it."

We're apparently in full agreement here—except that the employee has no idea what "improve your telephone answering skills" means. Maybe the manager isn't really sure, either.

If you're that manager, you have to think it through first and then say it straight.

- Answer the phone on the third ring or before.

- Respond pleasantly by identifying the company, giving your name, and adding, "How may I help you?"

- Offer to take a message, including the caller's name, phone number, purpose of the call, and best time to return the call.

Now you both know what you mean—and you'll both know whether the employee is actually doing it. And when you see improvement, you can also tell employees "Good job." That's also straight talk and gives them useful information on how they're doing.

When you're direct and clear, it simplifies the world for those you're speaking to and makes it much easier to them to feel motivated—they know what you have in mind.

 It's Not Rocket Science   Whatever form it takes, communication boils down to one human being talking to another human being with the goal of creating shared understanding. And the best way to share understanding is through conventional English.

Whether you're talking face to face, sending e-mail to a list of ten, or writing a report with a circulation in the thousands, you're still trying to communicate to one person at a time. You won't lose respect or authority if you sound like a human being when you do it.

In this lesson you learned how to use language that gets your message across clearly and helps your coworkers feel more motivated to work with you.

5

MEETINGS THAT MOTIVATE

In this lesson you'll learn how to conduct meetings that people will want to attend and that will increase motivation.

Ask folks to make a list of things they least like to do and chances are "go to a meeting" will rank right up there with "have root canal surgery" and "entertain my in-laws for a long weekend."

Most of us hate meetings. We avoid them when we can; resent them when we can't; and complain about them before, during, and after.

THE VALUE OF MEETINGS

Why have meetings? You could buy a lot of goodwill by never scheduling a meeting.

 tip

Meetings Can Be More than a Necessary Evil
You need meetings. Good things can happen then that simply can't happen with memos or e-mails or phone calls or one-on-one conversations. At meetings people can coordinate their work, and meetings give people a chance to help others and get help—all of which reinforces a person's motivation to perform well.

People get a sense of what's going on in other areas of the operation. Meetings put a human face on supervisors and colleagues with whom employees might not otherwise get a chance to interact. They help develop and maintain a sense of solidarity and shared mission and a spirit of cooperation. In a meeting:

- Everyone hears the same thing at the same time, removing some of the possibilities for miscommunication when information gets repeated.

- People ask for clarification.

- The speaker can read non-verbal clues (crossed arms, glazed eyes, eager nodding) to determine the level of interest and understanding in the group.

- Most important, when people interact, they get ideas they wouldn't have gotten otherwise.

Not seeing a lot of energy and interaction at your meetings now? Then let's look at when you call those meetings and how you lead them and the effect that has on motivation.

There are two schools of thought about holding meetings. (Well, three schools, if you count "Never!" as a school of thought.)

One school says regular meetings are a good idea, even if you don't have any pressing business to discuss. If you schedule regular meetings, this argument goes, folks gets used to the idea.

The best argument against holding regularly scheduled meetings finds support in one of the highest rules of leadership. That rule, simply stated: *Never waste people's time*—not with unnecessary meetings or memos or reports or committees or busy work.

If you waste their time, you steal a chunk of their lives. They'll resent you for it, and rightly so.

> **Don't Meet Just to Meet** Don't have a meeting if you don't have a real reason to meet that will help people perform better as individuals and as a group. Meetings that don't do that undermine motivation.

Once you start getting the group to work together toward common goals, however, you'll discover plenty of good reasons to have regular meetings. You shouldn't just respond to crises, after all. You should meet to conduct your business openly, with full participation by everyone.

So, schedule regular meetings. If you find a meeting date approaching and no real reason to meet (or compelling reasons not to), you can always cancel the meeting. Every time you lead a meeting, make it worth your coworkers' time and energy to be there.

CONDUCTING EFFECTIVE MEETINGS

There are several actions you can take to make sure meetings with your employees facilitate cooperation and improvement—in other words, to make sure your meetings motivate.

PREPARE YOURSELF

You really have to know your stuff to be able to present it to others, let alone explain it or lead a discussion on it. Do your homework.

Review your reason(s) for holding the meeting and the outcome(s) you want. The more focused and purposeful you are, the more on-target the meeting will be.

Picture the meeting running smoothly. You'll be a more confident leader, and positive thoughts surely make a better show than the disaster movie that might otherwise play in the theater of your mind.

PREPARE THE MEETING PLACE

Make sure you have the equipment you need, including things such as a flip chart and markers to record group input.

Think about seating arrangements. Put the participants in rows facing the front of the room if you want them to sit quietly and listen. (But if you do, better ask yourself why you need to drag them to a meeting to do it.) Put them around a table, and you've signaled to them that they're supposed to take an active part in the meeting, and you've made it much easier for them to do it.

PREPARE YOUR EMPLOYEES

Nothing kills a meeting quite so surely as a leader reading a long report or passing out thick copies of the report and asking folks to read them before the discussion starts. Now, that's a waste of time, and a good reason to loath meetings. It's also unfair, because it asks people to react to material without having a chance to think about it.

What do they need to know before the meeting? That's really two questions: What do *you* think they need to know? And what will *they* want to know? Attend to both questions. You're asking for your coworkers' time; think about what's in it for them. Process information from their point of view.

Get information into their hands a couple of days before the meeting. Sure, some won't read it. But some will, and they'll come prepared with questions and comments.

PREPARE AN AGENDA

You should also circulate an agenda a couple of days before the meeting. This doesn't need to be, and shouldn't be, fancy.

Agenda   A list of the items you plan to discuss, in the order you plan to discuss them.

Here are some tips for developing an effective agenda:

- Ask for agenda items from others well ahead of time.

- Plan for regular reports from folks with responsibility for and insight into various parts of the operation.

Get Down to Details   Be specific. An agenda that reads: "1. Announcements, 2. Old business, 3. New business, 4. Adjournment" is worse than no agenda. Make sure your agenda includes the topics you want to discuss, and it's a good idea to specify how much time you want to devote to those items.

- Emphasize action items and spell out recommendations you or others plan to make. Note if participants need to bring anything with them to the meeting.

- Don't put the controversial or otherwise difficult item(s) at the end of the agenda. Make sure there's enough time and energy for the important subjects.

- Be sure to indicate day, place, and time for the meeting on the agenda.

USE MEETINGS FOR TWO-WAY COMMUNICATION

Don't use meetings just for reading announcements and handing out reports that could have gone through interoffice mail.

Let everyone who will be affected by a decision discuss it. Make it clear whether you've put an item on the agenda for information or clarification purposes only or so that your employees can actually help make a decision.

SEEK CONSENSUS

Make sure everyone has a say. Don't let discussion become survival of the loudest. Seek out as many opinions as you can.

One of those diverse opinions can, of course, be yours. But if you're going to advocate a position, turn leadership of the discussion over to somebody else. The meeting leader shouldn't also be an advocate. That can be intimidating to others and can make them feel their say is not important.

Keep moving the group toward consensus, so that all those affected by the decision are comfortable with it and understand it. If you have to take a vote, the minority may feel angry or cheated and may never fully buy into the decision. You'll have much better results if you reach a position that everyone feels a part of.

Consensus Everyone in the group finds the decision acceptable and can commit to its implementation.

If you're the manager, it's still your call. You aren't giving away your authority. You couldn't give away the responsibility, even if you wanted to.

But you'll make a much better, more informed decision after discussing it with your colleagues, getting their input, and weighing their reasons. They'll be more willing to support that decision for having been heard and for having heard other points of view.

If you want them to feel motivated about the activities that are going to affect them, they have to be involved in decisions concerning these activities. Remember, you're seeking commitment, not compliance. People can't feel committed if they don't feel involved.

ESTABLISH GROUND RULES FOR DISCUSSION

Creating and maintaining an open, productive discussion may take some work, especially if some members of the group aren't used to such exchanges. Consider having the group establish some simple ground rules for discussion.

 Equality for All   The merit of a person's ideas doesn't depend on that person's rank or position in the organization.

Begin with the assumption that everyone at the meeting is responsible for his or her own behavior and also for the success of the meeting.

Here are a few ground rules other groups have found useful:

- Use "I" statements in sharing your perceptions. Not: "You're pressuring me." But: "I feel pressured by what you said."

- Address issues rather than people. Not: "Dan's idea about recycling styrofoam cups is idiotic." But: "I don't think recycling styrofoam cups is worth the time and effort."

- Come prepared to contribute.

- Listen to others' concerns. Don't interrupt.

- Avoid abusive language or tone. Don't yell.

 Stay Flexible   Don't adopt anybody else's list of rules. Each group should develop its own guidelines.

One member of the group should serve as facilitator for each discussion. The facilitator keeps the group on the subject at hand and following the ground rules. The job can rotate among all willing members of the group.

KEEP AND CIRCULATE A RECORD OF THE MEETING

Again, nothing fancy. Simply note:

- Who was present

- Topics discussed

- Decisions made and actions taken

- What still needs to be done

- When these items are supposed to be done

- Who is supposed to do these things

End with a reminder of the date, time, and place of the next meeting.

 Leave Out Dialogue   Minutes should not include dialogue from discussions. You'll do nothing but invite debate ("I never said that!"), and it's difficult, if not impossible, to get the conversation down accurately.

If you lead the meeting, you shouldn't also try to take the notes. You might try rotating this job, too.

Circulate the notes no more than five working days after the meeting to everyone who attended and everyone who wasn't there but wants or needs to know what happened.

FOLLOW UP

The biggest rap on meetings isn't that they're too long or boring. People feel ripped off by meetings when there's no follow up, nothing done about questions and suggestions, no decisions made, or decisions made in spite of, not because of, the discussion.

You're not done when the meeting adjourns—not by a long shot.

- If you said you'd get the information, get it.

- If you said you'd look into it, look into it.

- If you said you'd make a decision, make it.

- If you said you'd do it by Friday, do it by Friday.

Then tell them exactly what you did.

If you do everything right, and your meetings become good opportunities to exchange viewpoints and solve problems, folks will actually start enjoying them. But they'll never admit it, at least not to you. They'll go right on complaining about them.

That's okay. You may not get any prizes, but you'll get better decisions, stronger commitment to those decisions, and greater cooperative effort from everyone on the team.

When you look at it with those goals in mind, meetings aren't such a waste of time after all.

In this lesson you learned how to conduct meetings that people will want to attend and that will increase motivation.

TURN EVERY EMPLOYEE INTO A CREATIVE (AND MOTIVATED) PROBLEM SOLVER

In this lesson you'll learn how to turn on the motivation in employees to become creative problem solvers.

LET YOUR EMPLOYEES SOLVE THEIR (AND YOUR) PROBLEMS

Got a problem? Let the people closest to the problem solve it.

Sounds simple, doesn't it? Just good old horse sense. But that isn't how things usually get done in the workplace. More often, management takes the problem away from the worker, creates a committee, collects data, hires a consultant, issues a report, and imposes a "solution."

What does this do? Well, maybe it will solve the problem and maybe it won't. One thing it will do for certain, however, is to tell employees you don't trust them. And when you don't trust them, they stop trusting themselves and stop feeling very good about their employer. Anytime there is a lack of trust, it will negatively affect employee motivation.

Or maybe the problem never even gets addressed because managers don't address it. And the people on the front lines don't feel empowered to do anything about it—even though they may be best qualified to discover problems and to solve them. If your employees aren't into problem solving, you might wonder why.

Hint: It isn't because they aren't smart enough or that they checked their brains at the door when they punched in or because they don't care.

Let Them Know You Care   Employees don't volunteer solutions because they don't think managers want to hear them. They don't get recognized or rewarded for making suggestions. They may even feel actively discouraged to do this because nothing ever happens when they do come forward with a new idea or a solution for a perceived problem. Nothing kills an employee's motivation to solve problems like a lack of response from management.

Don't establish a committee or create a task force or set up a commission. Don't hire a consultant. Ask the employees! Then reward them when they come through with suggestions. A bonus would be nice, of course. Public recognition in the company newsletter or at the next meeting is great and doesn't cost anybody a cent. But the best reward is to listen to and consider the idea.

BRAINSTORMING

Get your folks together for a brainstorming session. Keep it short, and keep it moving. Establish two important ground rules before you start.

Explore All Options When searching for solutions, don't look for the "right way." Instead, play "How many ways?" Look for lots of potential solutions and then select one that might make sense and refine it until it does.

- It doesn't matter where an idea comes from.

  Uncouple the idea from the person who had it. Sometimes the person who had an idea doesn't want others to change or add to it, and that hinders the brainstorming session. Make sure that everyone understands that all ideas are the group's to refine, modify, and build on.

- Say "Yes" to every idea.

  Don't reject any idea. Don't criticize, edit, or amend it. Just receive it, clarify it if need be, and note it. (Somebody should be at the chalkboard or flip chart for this duty.)

You can't judge the quality of the idea yet. The stupid, far-out, crazy, impractical notion may turn out to be just what you need. It only seemed crazy because you hadn't thought of it before. And even the stupid idea can trigger the next idea, which can lead you where you want to go.

Avoid these classic put-downs, guaranteed to chase away original thinking (and kill motivation to deal with problems in the first place):

- *If it ain't broke, don't fix it.* Nonsense. It "works" now. How can it work better?

- *We've never done it that way before.* Good. We were trying to come up with *new* ideas, right?

- *I'm not comfortable with that.* Also good. New ideas often push us out of our comfort zones.

- *You're no authority.* So what? Ideas aren't responsible for who gets them. And ideas don't respect any caste system.

- *The boss will never go for it.* The boss doesn't have to go for it yet. We're just getting ideas. Later we can apply our creative thinking to ways to sell the idea to the brass.

You aren't looking for the "right answer," remember. It isn't lost, waiting for you to find it. You're out to create answers, as many as possible, the more the better. Just because someone's idea doesn't sound "right" to you the first time you hear it doesn't mean it can't work.

Look Positively on Ideas   Stop playing "devil's advocate." Start playing "angel's advocate" instead. Think about what you can do to make an idea work rather than why it won't work.

The great advertising executive, Alex Osborne, who originated the term "brainstorming," said it best: "If you want to have a good idea, have *lots* of ideas." You'll select and judge and implement later. First you need a lot of ideas to select from.

We all learn to say "No" automatically. And "Yes, but..." comes real easy to us, too. Teach yourself and your coworkers to say "Yes, and..." instead.

In the creative process, there's literally no such thing as a mistake. You can't be wrong if you're only trying to generate as long a list of ideas as you can.

No Put-Downs Allowed   Here's another approach to be open to a new idea: Never put it down. Think of three things good about it and then you can express your concerns. Finally, deal with the concerns until you have refined the idea into a solution.

Take your cue from Thomas Edison, who reportedly tried more than 700 elements before he found one that would function as a filament for a light bulb. When asked how he endured all those failures, he said that none of them were failures. He had found 700 things that didn't work.

THE TALE OF THE STUDENT AND THE BAROMETER

Here's a classic example of creative problem-solving.

Our student (let's call him Jim) fully intends to do his physics homework. But something better comes up, and Jim doesn't get that chapter on barometric pressure read.

That, of course, brings on a pop quiz in class the next day (just as washing your car surely makes it rain).

The teacher poses a simple question: "Using a barometer, how would you determine the height of the Empire State Building?"

Jim is sunk. He vaguely remembers a formula involving barometric pressure and altitude. If he knew the formula, he'd simply take his barometer, note the pressure, jump into the elevator on the ground floor, and ride to the top of the Empire State Building. He'd then note the new pressure, compute the difference, plug it into the formula, and have his answer.

Except that he doesn't know the formula.

He can bag it or bluff it, turn in an empty test paper or come up with some answer that might earn him partial credit. Being a clever guy, Jim comes up with not one but several possible solutions:

- You could drop the barometer off the top of the building, he reasons, and time how long it takes to hit the ground. (Nothing in the question indicated you couldn't use a stopwatch, and nobody said the barometer had to be in one piece when you got done.)

- You could tie a rope to the barometer, lower it off the top of the building, and when it hit the sidewalk, measure the length of rope.

- You could even climb the side of the building, counting off the height in barometer lengths, and multiply by the length of the barometer.

But Jim saved his best solution for last.

- You could find the architect who designed the building and offer to give him your barometer if he'll tell you exactly how tall the building is.

None of these is the "right" answer, by the book. But in real life there usually isn't a book and seldom a single right way to find the answer. There's only trying to figure out a solution that works.

Questions, Questions The question you ask will determine the answer you find. Ask the question in as many ways as you can.

The good folks who make Pringles potato chips got hung up trying to develop a better bag—one that would keep the chips fresh and prevent crumbling and breaking. The breakthrough came when they asked a better question: how to create a better *container*. The broader question let them play with more possibilities, try out more silly solutions. One of those silly suggestions, the kind of vacuum-sealed tube used to store tennis balls, turned into the first great breakthrough in potato chip packaging since the invention of the chip itself.

Brainstorming only works in an atmosphere of cooperation and shared purpose. If I define my self-interest narrowly, so that I need to receive credit for everything I do or say while looking only to improve my own status, I won't share ideas or help you improve yours.

As a leader, you must discourage this sort of territorial marking. Break down the barriers between "subdepartments" by defining job responsibility broadly, by creating fluid job descriptions, and by rewarding cooperative effort. Encourage people to work together to solve problems and celebrate breakthroughs. This is how you help employees feel motivated to deal with problems through creativity and enthusiasm.

In this lesson you learned how to turn on the motivation in employees to help them become creative problem solvers.

7

WHEN WORK IS ITS OWN REWARD

In this lesson you'll learn that when people have work they feel is right for them, they will be naturally motivated to perform well.

We do what we do because of what happens when we do it. If we like what happens when we do something, then we are likely to continue doing it.

Work creates its own reward when it meets three conditions:

- People like what they're doing.

- They see the importance of their tasks.

- They do the job well in their opinion and in the opinion of others that they respect.

Under those conditions, workers will feel satisfaction and a sense of accomplishment—the two strongest motivators there are. When that happens, we call it positive reinforcement.

Positive Reinforcement When an action produces pleasure or removes pain. When that happens, the action reinforces itself, increasing the likelihood that the individual will want to do it again.

Watch a kid throwing a tennis ball against a garage door. He's "working" at learning how to throw a ball straight and fast. And maybe he's also dreaming of pitching in the major leagues one day.

Will he ever make it to "The Show"? Probably not. Few kids who throw tennis balls against garage doors ever do. And even if he does make it, he won't be able to realize his dream for years. How could anything so unlikely and so far off motivate him to throw that tennis ball over and over again now?

It can't. He's throwing the tennis ball because he's having fun doing it right now. He's imagining he's blazing his famous fastball past a lunging Darryl Strawberry or getting Juan Gonzalez to swing at and miss his sneaky curve ball—all to the roar of the 50,000 fans jamming the stadium of his mind.

Throwing the ball against the garage door is self-reinforcing for the kid who enjoys doing it. But if that kid would rather be inside playing computer games, no amount of urging or cajoling or ordering from Dad can ever make throwing that ball seem like fun.

THE PARABLE OF THE POP MACHINE

You're thirsty. Water just won't do it. You want something cold and tasty. You spot a pop machine, slam a buck into the slot, push the button, and a 20-ounce bottle of liquid refreshment clangs and thuds its way out of the chute. You twist the cap slowly and take a long swig. Ahhhhh.

Desire motivated action. Action brought reinforcement, immediate and appropriate. You got rid of a negative (thirst) and produced a positive (good taste). Your action has been reinforced. Next time you feel thirsty and want something cold and tasty, there's a good chance you'll head back to that pop machine.

Keep the Reinforcement Coming   Want to get folks to use your pop machine? You don't have to instruct them or order them. No point in writing a memo on the benefits of using the pop machine. Forget the pep rally equating "team spirit" with using the pop machine. Don't try gold stars on the performance chart every time somebody uses the pop machine. All you need to do is service and refill the pop machine, so the cool refreshing drink comes out when the buck goes in. The action reinforces itself.

How does all this apply to the workplace? Simple. If you want your coworkers and employees to feel motivated, the best thing you can do is match the worker to the kind of work he or she really enjoys and is good at. Then make sure they have the tools and support to do well.

But what happens if I put my hard-earned buck in the pop machine, push the button, and nothing comes out the chute? I pound on the machine, push all the buttons, maybe even deliver a swift kick to the offending hunk of metal. Then I'll remember never to put another dollar in that machine.

That's an example of the principle of extinction.

Extinction   When what you do doesn't get what you expect or want, pretty soon you stop doing it.

If the work isn't self-reinforcing—and if you don't do something to reinforce it—you're going to have a tough time getting anybody to feel motivated to do it. And if they aren't motivated, these tasks are unlikely to get done.

No Reinforcement, No Action If a worker's actions aren't reinforced, the worker will stop performing those actions. This isn't laziness. It's human nature. You react the same way. So make sure you reinforce actions that contribute to getting the job done.

FIRST POP PRINCIPLE OF MOTIVATION

When somebody puts a buck in the slot, they want something to drink—not a pat on the back, a word of praise, or a positive performance review.

There's nothing wrong with sincere praise for a job well done. In fact, there's not nearly enough of it in the workplace these days, and it can be a powerful reward. But even sincere, timely praise from someone else isn't as effective as the positive reinforcement that comes from personally knowing you have done your best and gotten results that you're pleased with.

Needed: Self Reinforcement Self reinforcement is stronger than external reward. Create a situation in which people can be successful at their work and feel good about it, and there will be self reinforcement.

SECOND POP PRINCIPLE OF MOTIVATION

People want different things to drink.

Some folks love pop. They'll naturally head for the pop machine. But some folks want café latté. They'll walk right past the pop machine on their way out the door to the local Steep 'N Sip. Café latté drinkers won't be motivated by the presence of a pop machine in the break room.

Play to Their Strengths   Find out what folks like to do and are good at and let them do it. The way to find out what they like to do is to ask them and watch them.

Watch what your coworkers do when they have a choice. Note what they do well. Use this knowledge to match worker with right work.

Suppose Sam and Sally work for you and half their job entails handling phone inquiries for you and the other half involves filing. Sam hears opportunity every time the phone rings, but dreads filing. When Sally's phone rings, she curses under her breath. She would much rather be doing the filing.

Sam answers the phone with a cheerful greeting. He greets the question or complaint with genuine concern and a desire to help. If he doesn't have the answer, he'll find it and get back to the caller promptly.

With Sally, it's service with a snarl—especially if someone calls before she's had her morning café latté.

Do you really want Sally answering half of your phone calls? You have to be fair, don't you? Answering phone inquiries is part of Sam and Sally's job descriptions. It wouldn't be fair to make Sam do all the phone work. Sally should carry her fair share. And you, as manager, must assert your authority by making her do it.

You can do that if you really want to. Give Sally a quota of calls to answer. Praise her every time you see her doing it well (positive reinforcement). Write her up every time she cusses out a potential customer (negative reinforcement). Send her to a workshop to enhancing her phone skills.

You'll have asserted your authority. But Sally will still hate answering the phone, and now she'll resent you, too. And she'll go right on doing a lousy job—while Sam mutters his way through the "damn filing" Sally would rather be doing.

Or you can let Sam answer the phone and let Sally handle the filing.

It's your call. You can come on tough, or you can be smart. If you're smart, you'll end up with two motivated employees who enjoy their work and are good at it.

THIRD POP PRINCIPLE OF MOTIVATION

Reinforcement must be immediate.

Let's take one more trip to that pop machine, where a sign on the front advises you to "Read this before making your selection." So you do.

"Thank you for selecting one of our carbonated beverages. Please insert dollar bill in slot and push appropriate button. Then type your name and address on the keyboard provided to the left of the machine. Your selection will be delivered to your home or place of business within six working days of this transaction. Have a nice day, and enjoy your beverage."

Crazy, right? You don't want something to drink in six days. You want it now. So you stick your buck back in your pocket or purse and look for another machine, one without the six-day waiting period.

Nobody would set up a vending machine with that sort of lag time. But lots of companies and organizations try to reinforce good work habits that way. You do a great job, day in and day out, but only hear about it on your quarterly, semi-annual, or even annual evaluation. You do some really great work in February and get some notice for it the following January. That doesn't do much for motivation.

On the other hand, if an employee sends you a memo with a good idea, make a copy of it and write "I like this! Good work!" You've given the employee positive reinforcement that helps assure this individual will feel motivated to keep trying to come up with more good ideas. Imagine the difference if this employee never heard from you or maybe gets a short note a month later. Since you didn't get back quickly, it seems that you probably don't care that much, so neither will the employee.

SOMETHING THAT DOESN'T REINFORCE GOOD PERFORMANCE

Am I saying that quarterly performance reviews and yearly bonuses are ineffective as reinforcers in the workplace? I'm saying more than that. Quarterly performance reviews and yearly bonuses aren't just bad reinforcers. They aren't really reinforcers at all.

You probably have to perform, as well as receive, reviews, just as I do. You have to document performance, comply with regulations, have something on file. And that performance review, if you do it well, can serve as an effective reward for good work, as we'll see in the next lesson. But it will never be as powerful as the satisfaction of doing work you enjoy.

In this lesson you learned that when people have work they feel is right for them, they will be naturally motivated to perform well.

8

REWARD WHAT YOU WANT

In this lesson you'll learn how to use rewards to reinforce the motivation of your coworkers to do what you want them to do.

REWARDS AND MOTIVATION TO PERFORM

More than a decade ago, Michael LeBoeuf revealed "the greatest management principle in the world": Reward what you want.

It's really that simple.

If the work itself doesn't contain its own reinforcement, then you as manager should try to attach an appropriate reward to the work.

But you already *do* reward them, you say. They get paid! Shouldn't that be enough?

The paycheck is surely a reward and an incentive. But we don't live by paychecks—and the bread they buy—alone. We work best when we feel appreciated and respected.

Better Than Nothing Reinforcement is better than reward. But reward is better—lots better—than nothing. If you do it right.

BE CAREFUL IN USING REWARDS

But there are dangers involved in relying on rewards to motivate high performance.

 Be More than Automatic Automatic rewards, such as annual step-increases in pay, do nothing to reinforce particular actions. If you think they do, you will be disappointed.

We like the hike in pay. We just don't associate it with anything specific that we do.

Even if the reward is linked to specific job performance, it still may defeat the purpose of rewarding and thus reinforcing specific behavior. That happens when the reward becomes an end in itself, separate from the job being rewarded.

For example, if I work only to get the positive performance review I need to earn my merit pay at the end of the fiscal year, I may slack off after each review period. If I'm performing only to impress my supervisor, what will keep me working when the supervisor isn't around?

REWARDS THAT MOTIVATE

So, what kind of reward *will* work to reinforce motivation?

To be effective, a reward should be:

- Linked to specific performance
- Timely
- Frequent

Even if you tie the yearly pay increase to some sort of merit standard, it may not motivate nearly as effectively as a little something extra in the pay envelope at the end of the week. The longer you delay the reward, separating it from the action being rewarded, the less effective it will be as a way to reinforce motivation.

Effort Counts, Too   Waiting to reward until the job's all done means you're only rewarding results, not effort. That might sound like a solid principle; after all, it's results that count, right? But often the success or failure of any project depends on variables outside the individual worker's control. So good effort never gets rewarded.

A coworker comes up with a great idea or performs heroic extra effort. But the project never really amounts to anything. No reward for that worker? Okay, but don't expect him or her to keep making the heroic efforts. You've done nothing to show your appreciation for those efforts, and that means you've successfully extinguished them.

Reward Effort   Celebrate effort, not just outcome. If you do that, you are telling people that seeking to do the job well and learning from their experience is important to you. This reinforces a person's motivation to try hard to do well.

WHAT MAKES THE MOST EFFECTIVE REWARD?

Some folks love a surprise party in their honor. For others, being the center of that kind of attention is painful and embarrassing. The gift turns into a punishment.

As the fabled Green Bay Packers coach, Vince Lombardi, once said, "Nothing is more unequal than the equal treatment of unequals." (I like that quote a lot better than that one about winning not being everything.)

 Familiarity Helps   The better you know the worker, the more likely it is you'll be able to reward that worker effectively. You will be able to better identify with that worker and he or she with you.

There's no rule that says you can't ask your coworkers what sorts of incentives they'd prefer.

TANGIBLE REWARDS

There are two categories of rewards: tangibles and trophies. Let's start with tangibles.

 Tangible Rewards   Rewards with actual value. They include a merit pay raise or bonus, of course, but also may take many other forms. Even a trophy, if the employee can hock it or melt it down for precious metals, is a tangible reward.

Ben & Jerry's Homemade Inc. lets employees take home three pints of ice cream every day. Anheuser-Busch employees get vouchers good for two free cases of beer a month, as do workers at Pete's Wicked Brewing Company of Palo Alto, California. Robert Mondavi gives each employee a case of wine at the end of every quarter. Rubbermaid Inc. awards employees "rubber bucks" for a job well done, redeemable for goods at a company store. Such tokens of appreciation tell employees the company cares about them. When employees know this, they are more likely to identify their welfare with the company and be more motivated to perform well.

Here are some more examples:

- Benjamin Moore lets employees buy paint at whole-sale prices and then goes one better, sending crews out to two employees each year to paint their houses for free.

- Eli Lilly & Company gives employees free Prozac— but only if they have a prescription, of course. The health plan covers 100 percent of any drug Lilly makes.

TROPHY AWARDS

A small trophy for the desk, a certificate for the wall, a mention in the newsletter, all can be important, as can a cookie from the corner bakery or a cup of hot coffee waiting at the desk in the morning after an overtime session the day before.

 Trophy Reward   A reward that has little or no cash value but has symbolic meaning to the one who receives it. It says "job well done" and is another way to reinforce a person's motivation to do a good job.

Despite our attempts to save it, you can't take time to the bank. But time off can be as powerful as any monetary reward. Do the job fast and well and I get an afternoon off? Watch my dust!

A simple "Way to go!" at the right moment can do wonders. A handwritten thank-you note doesn't cost the company anything except a bit of your time, and it won't bring anything on the open market (unless your signature has celebrity value, of course). But it may have great worth to the recipient. Jan Carlzon, President of Scandinavian Airlines, sends personal thank yous all the time.

 Negativism Stings   It takes four "way to gos" to balance out the negative impact of just one "You really screwed up." Remember, praise should be frequent and sincere.

A thank you takes on even greater symbolic value when coupled with public recognition. The Burroughs Company celebrates workers' triumphs with a posted "Brag Sheet."

Verbal praise at the next staff meeting might be a great inducement for some—but remember, for some, such praise would be embarrassing. So use it with discretion. If it embarrasses a person to get public praise, then do it in private.

 Asking for Trouble   Naming an "Employee of the Week" (or month or year) may have considerable symbolic value for the winner and may even create incentive, but it's a dangerous practice and may backfire, as we'll see in the next lesson.

If a promotion carries with it an increase in pay, it has both trophy and tangible value. A change in title and duties without a pay raise may provide considerable symbolic value—or it may be seen as a punishment: more work and more responsibility for the same old salary.

Promote Promotions   Any promotion can have symbolic value in terms of increased prestige if you let everyone know about it. Look for opportunities to celebrate promotions publicly.

Not all of the symbolic rewards have to come from you. Peer reward is as effective as it is underused. Praise from the one who works shoulder-to-shoulder with you—and thus understands exactly what excellent performance actually requires—may be more powerful than anything a supervisor can render.

But what about reward's other side, correction and criticism? Surely that must have a place in your tool chest as an effective manager and leader.

Read on. We've talked about the carrot. In the next lesson we'll take on the whip.

In this lesson you learned how to use rewards to reinforce the motivation of your coworkers to do what you want them to do.

9

COACHING AND MOTIVATION

In this lesson you'll learn why criticism and competition undermine motivation while coaching and cooperation enhance it.

How would you like to manage a department where your folks did the job on time, every time—because they know how to perform and are motivated to do so? You'd probably like that just fine, right?

You can create that kind of workplace.

But you won't do it with criticism and competition. You'll get there through coaching and cooperation.

Let Clarke Stallworth tell you how.

A COACHING EXAMPLE

Sometimes the best way to gain an understanding of something is to learn from stories about others. Here's one such story.

BEING A BOSS, NOT A COACH

By his own admission, Stallworth was one mean S.O.B. As managing editor of the *Birmingham* (Alabama) *News,*

Stallworth rode herd on a constantly changing band of reporters, many of them rookies. He'd give an assignment, get the copy in, and tear it to shreds.

"I'd just rip it up big-time," he admits.

He knew how it was supposed to be written, he reasoned, so he'd fix it.

"They hated me for it," he says.

But that's what an editor's supposed to do, right? And nobody said being a manager was supposed to be a popularity contest.

That's what Stallworth thought, too. But he slowly became aware of a rather fundamental problem with his system—it didn't work.

The copy his reporters turned in didn't get any better, despite all of Stallworth's revisions. Reporters made the same mistakes over and over, as if they were actively resisting Stallworth's efforts to show them how it ought to be done.

They resisted, all right, right up until they quit. Stallworth's reporters didn't tend to stick around long. He'd get them broken in, and they'd move on.

Everybody—Especially You—Is a Critic Your coworkers learn only one thing from your criticism. They learn that you're a critic.

BEING A COACH, NOT A BOSS

Stallworth couldn't seem to change his reporters. So he changed himself. He stopped being an editor and became a coach.

Instead of just sending reporters out on assignment, Stallworth began talking them through the assignment first, discussing what they ought to be looking for and what questions they ought to be asking.

Before a reporter wrote the story, Stallworth discussed what the "nut" or essence of it ought to be. During these sessions, Stallworth mostly asked questions. Under his quiet prodding, the reporter came up with the answers.

But the biggest change came when the reporter filed the story. Instead of tearing it to shreds and handing the pieces back, as he had always done, Stallworth sat down with the reporter and asked two questions:

- "What's right with it?"
- "How can you make it better?"

The reporter did most of the talking and Stallworth did a lot of listening. The reporter also did the rewriting. The story got better, the reporter learned the craft, and, perhaps most important, the story remained the reporter's and not the editor's. In other words, they had a win-win situation that enhanced rather than defeated the reporter's motivation to get better.

"Before, when I was 'fixing' copy, I was taking it away from them," Stallworth explains. "By the time I got done with it, they didn't care about it any more."

 It's Their Work   "Fix" it for them, and the work becomes yours. Let them fix it, and it remains theirs— along with the pride, the satisfaction, and the sustained motivation that comes from doing it right.

Stallworth's new method took a little more time—in the beginning. But he got that time and more back by no longer having to rip up stories or break in new reporters after the old ones had quit.

"I thought the copy was the most important thing," he concludes. "But I was wrong. The most important thing is the reporter." Of course, when he focuses on the reporter, the reporter feels motivated to be deserving of that focus and is motivated to get things right.

It's the Worker, Not the Work   As a leader, your most important product isn't the work. It's the growth of the worker.

SOME LESSONS IN COACHING

Stallworth made this system work in the newsroom of a daily newspaper, one of the most pressure-filled and deadline-driven workplaces on earth. If he could make it work there, you can make it work in your workplace, too.

Stallworth's ability to get peak performance from his reporters didn't come from his title or from any assertion of his authority. The power came from his knowledge and the way he used that knowledge to encourage growth in the reporters working with him.

You're More Important Than Rewards   More than money or praise or any other reward you can give, your ability to lead and influence the motivation of others comes from your ability to help them do their work better.

Stallworth liberated his reporters by demonstrating his respect for their intelligence and ability. He kept the creative process where it belonged, with the creator. By doing so, he created an atmosphere in which reporters could learn—not by just taking in information but by expanding their capacity to produce results.

Less Control, More Control   The phrase "quality control" is a contradiction. You want quality? Loosen your control. The more controls you apply, the less real control you have.

Trust your coworkers' judgment. Expect the best from them. Provide the tools, knowledge, and feedback they need. Then hold them accountable for the results. Ask them what they learned from the process. Ask them how they could do it better next time.

Set reasonable goals, high enough to challenge but within reach. Set many goals rather than few, increasing opportunities for success along the way. Explain each goal as clearly and specifically as possible.

Then step back and let them work. Your coworkers have the right to try and fail. That's the only way they can learn.

Criticize Privately, Praise Publicly   If you need to step in and offer constructive criticism, do it in private, one on one. But when it's time to hand out the credit, hire a band and throw a party.

WHY YOU SHOULDN'T NAME AN "EMPLOYEE OF THE MONTH"

Suppose you decide to motivate your staff by designating an "Employee of the Month." You can award merit points. You can establish competitive goals. You can draw names out of a hat. The result will be the same: You create one winner and a whole bunch of losers. Keep the competition honest, and you'll get the same few winners over and over. Rotate the award so that everybody has a turn to win and you render it meaningless.

 One Winner, Many Losers When you set up a competition, you create one happy winner—and lots of unhappy losers. And you can imagine what that does to motivation.

You'll run into the same problem with competitive merit pay schedules. I worked in a setting where everybody got a base raise each year, and workers were ranked for "special merit" above and beyond the baseline. Everybody should have been happy, since everybody got at least some raise (the baseline), and some folks got even more. But year after year almost every worker, including the ones with the fattest raises, complained that the system was arbitrary and unfair. The folks at the bottom of the scale—invariably the same folks year after year—felt bitter and cheated. Or worse, they felt like losers.

CREATING WINNERS

As a coach you can recognize excellence and develop winners without creating "losers" by establishing objective standards.

The Mary Kay Cosmetics system of payoffs—culminating in the famous pink Cadillac—rewards success, celebrating winners without creating losers. You work against a fixed scale of rewards, not against the other salespeople. You earn the points, you get the rewards, without taking anybody else down by comparison.

The reward works because:

- It flows from and is linked to performance.

- It's positive and certain.

- It occurs close enough to the performance to be meaningful as reinforcement.

If you want your coworkers to work together for a common goal, reward cooperation rather than competition. Create a challenge for the whole group. When the group achieves the goal, all share in the credit and the reward. If the group falls short, they fall short together.

But won't such cooperative effort sap initiative? Aren't we by our very nature competitive? I doubt it. All talk about the "law of the jungle" and "survival of the fittest" aside, you can make as good a case that mankind is by nature cooperative as you can for the contrary.

If your organization functions in a competitive marketplace—and most of them do—focus your colleagues' energies on effectively beating the competition, not each other.

You want your crew to outrace all the others, yes, but they'll only do so if you get them all rowing together.

In this lesson you learned why criticism and competition undermine motivation, while coaching and cooperation enhance it.

10

CORRECTING MISTAKES WITHOUT DESTROYING MOTIVATION

In this lesson you'll learn how to handle your coworkers' mistakes without destroying their motivation.

"Zero tolerance for error."

There's one of the more chilling phrases to come out of the quality movement in America. What do you do about mistakes? Don't tolerate them.

There, now. Wasn't that easy? Just say to "no" to screw-ups.

But you know it doesn't happen that way. Well-meaning, competent, qualified, and highly motivated people make mistakes.

MISTAKES: THEY HAPPEN

One of those well-meaning, competent, qualified, highly motivated mistake-makers is you.

Refusing to tolerate error sounds a lot like refusing to recognize it when it happens, or finding somebody to blame for it, or explaining why a mistake isn't really a mistake.

Learn from Mistakes   Here's a basic truth I learned from my editor friend, John Woods: Mistakes are always value judgments rendered after the fact. Nobody intentionally makes a mistake. Think of it for what it is: a learning experience.

None of these are productive strategies for dealing with the mistakes that people will inevitably commit. Further, they all negatively affect a person's motivation to do things right because they communicate the following:

- You don't know what's right or wrong behavior.

- You want to find a scapegoat when something goes wrong.

- You're willing to tolerate mediocrity if someone can come up with an excuse.

So, what *do* you do when somebody messes up big-time—and you don't want to undermine his or her motivation to perform?

Before you decide, remember these three fundamental truths about human nature:

- Your coworkers are trying to do it right.

- They'll give you what they get from you.

- They'll model your behavior.

THE CASE FOR SAYING NOTHING

Your best response to a coworker's error may be no response at all. This is the case when:

- The worker is aware that he or she made a mistake.

- The mistake was the result of lack of knowledge or skills and the individual can learn from the experience.

- The worker knows how to do it right.

But as the manager, don't you have to respond—if for no other reason than to show that you're in charge?

In a word, no. You don't ever need to assert your authority by pointing out something that your coworker already knows and regrets.

If you feel that you do need to say something about a coworker's fluff, first review exactly what you hope to accomplish.

First, you want the worker to be aware of the mistake. If they don't know they've made one, they're liable to go right on making it. If a worker knows it's a mistake, they'll try to correct it themselves, without waiting for you to tell them.

Second, you want the worker to fix it if they can. And they want the opportunity to make it right if possible, without you stepping in to do it for them.

Third, you want them to do it right next time.

That should be *all* you want. Therefore, say nothing and watch to see if this person gets it right next time. If not, then you might intervene as a helper, not a critic. If he or she does do it right, you might want make a compliment, noting that you appreciate his or her efforts.

Three Things You Should Never Do to Employees Who Make Mistakes

There are three things you should not do to employees who make mistakes if you want them to remain motivated and committed employees.

1. *Don't try to make them pay for their mistake.* They've already paid. They're embarrassed, and they've lost ground on their work goals. If they know they've made a mistake and are trying to correct it and you come along and make them feel worse, all it says is that you don't care about them or their feelings. You can imagine what that does to their motivation.

2. *Don't make them say they're sorry.* Of course they're sorry. And the mistake wasn't directed at you. Don't make a personal issue out of it.

3. *Don't "make an example" out of them.* You won't be teaching the lesson you intend. When you reprimand a worker in front of their peers, you're telling everyone within earshot that the way to get your attention is to screw up. You're telling them to be cautious, to avoid taking risks that might lead to mistakes, to play not to lose rather than to play to win. Most of all, you're teaching them to live down to your low expectations of them.

But won't you look soft if you don't give them a good chewing out? You've got to show who's boss, right? After all, like the man said, "Nice guys finish last."

That man was Leo Durocher, and he never even said it. A sportswriter twisted Durocher's off-hand observation that the rival Brooklyn Dodgers were a bunch of nice guys but that they were probably going to finish last that year.

Nobody ever accused "Leo the Lip" of being a nice guy, but he managed to finish last in 1966, guiding the Chicago Cubs to a miserable 59-103 record.

Effectiveness Counts   Don't worry about being tough—or nice. Be effective, meaning take actions that will help people perform well without undermining their motivation to do so.

SOME WAYS TO HELP EMPLOYEES WHEN THEY MAKE MISTAKES

Here's how to make winners out of yourself and your co-workers when they make mistakes.

1. If they are not aware of the problem, tell them now. And give them directions and support for improving.

   The longer you wait, the harder it gets to deliver the message, and the less effect that message has. Don't store up notes for the weekly staff meeting or the quarterly performance review. Tell them as soon as possible. This nips the problem in the bud and provides support for doing things right. It communicates "I care and want to help you." And that helps sustain a person's motivation to perform well.

2. Tell them before you tell anybody else.

   A worker has the right to hear it from you before they hear it from the grapevine. People don't like to be talked about behind their back.

3. Tell them in private.

   If you humiliate an individual in public, they'll resent you, and they'll get defensive. They'll be motivated from this—motivated to get back at you. A private conversation that focuses on helping the person perform better, on the other hand, invites real learning and growth.

4. Separate the sin from the sinner.

    Making a mistake isn't the same as *being* a mistake. A person may have fouled up, but that doesn't mean he or she is incompetent or ill-willed.

5. Ask and listen.

    If you're doing all the talking, you're not learning a thing. It's not just a matter of getting "their side of the story." A worker who makes a mistake might not even have a "side." See the situation as they see it. Find out why the mistake happened. You might discover that the real source of the mistake is deeper in the system than what one employee did.

6. Accentuate the positive.

    Find the right in what the employee has done. Stress the positive nature of your conversation—awareness and problem-solving. This will help the employee to be positive as well.

7. Say it straight.

    Here's where real toughness—and real courage— enter in. If you've got bad news, say it in simple, direct language. The more you try to soften the message, the less forceful it becomes and the less sincere you appear. If employees understand the urgency of doing things right, and if they understand that your job is to support that, they will share your sense of urgency and want to work with you. If you're a supervisor, your job is not to sit around correcting employees. It's to take actions that facilitate and sustain high performance—and motivation.

8. Talk from a sense of shared purpose.

   You may be the boss, but everybody is working for the same goals. Everyone wants to do their jobs well, and they want to help the organization fulfill its mission. You win together, or lose together.

9. Don't use comparisons.

   The work is either right or wrong, but it isn't right or wrong in comparison to somebody else's work. Measure people's performance against objective standards.

10. Pinpoint active behaviors.

    You say: "Don't ever, *ever* put the invoice inside the packing crate!" And your coworker says: "Okay. I got it. No invoice in the packing crate. So, what *do* I do with the damn thing?"

    Don't just tell employees what not to do. Tell them what they're supposed to do—and be specific. Tell employees to put the invoice in the envelope and tape the envelope to the outside of the crate, where it belongs. Or show them how, if that's required—and don't forget the positive feedback when they do it right.

When you need to redirect a worker's efforts, make sure you cover these bases:

- Tell them what they did wrong and why it was wrong.

- Tell them what you want them to do instead—and make sure they know how to do it.

- Follow up. Tell them when they do it right, and remind them in a supportive way when they don't.

You want to show them how tough you really are? Never make a colleague take the fall for you. If you screwed up, say so. Then tell them what you're going to do to make it right and to make sure it doesn't happen again.

The bad supervisor talks tough to the people under her and curries favor with those higher up the line. The good supervisor treats people under her with courtesy and respect and saves the tough talk for the bosses.

A good supervisor fights for, not with, his or her coworkers and helps them continuously learn from their experience to get better.

In this lesson you learned how to handle your coworkers' inevitable mistakes without destroying their motivation.

11

TIME MANAGEMENT FOR MOTIVATION

In this lesson you'll learn seven tips for how to better manage time, get more important things done, and feel more motivated.

All of the people who work with you have one thing in common: They're all too busy. And so are you. There just aren't enough hours in the day. No matter how hard you try, you can't get it all done.

ARE YOU BUSY OR ARE YOU PRODUCTIVE?

You're all trying to manage time wisely, learning to do two, three, four things at once, anything to stuff more productive activity into a day. You use calendars and day planners and to-do lists. You prioritize. You buy gadgets to help you work faster, think faster, even look and listen faster.

We tell each other to "work smarter, not harder" so we can "do more with less."

We're living as if life were a football game, and we're caught in the two-minute no-huddle hurry-up offense. And yet, to paraphrase the great old pitcher/philosopher Satchel Paige, the "hurrieder" we go, the "behinder" we get. Result: frustration and compromised motivation.

Maybe it's time to take a different approach to time.

Slow Down and Do Things Right   If trying to speed everybody up doesn't seem to be working, try slowing them down just a bit, so they can focus on doing the right things in the right way.

Instead of struggling to do *more* things, let's work on doing the *right* things.

FIRST PRINCIPLE OF TIME MANAGEMENT FOR MOTIVATION

Never waste their time.

"Don't ever let the man catch you standing around," a wise old laborer named Andy advised me the day I started work as a construction laborer. "You've got to look busy."

So I learned to keep in constant motion. On days when there was nothing to do, I'd pick up litter, hammer nails out of boards, sweep the sidewalks—and then turn around and sweep the same dirt back the other way.

Those were the bad days. Time crawls when you're thinking of ways to make it pass. I think I know why the supervisor would get mad if he caught any of us leaning on our shovels. Our lack of motion challenged his authority. It was his job to keep us moving. If we weren't moving, it meant he wasn't doing his job.

How about you? Does the sight of one of your coworkers standing idle threaten you? If so, resist the temptation to assign busy work. You waste their time making them do the work and your time thinking the work up for them, supervising them while they do it, and pretending to care about it when it's done. None of which does much to make them— or you—feel very motivated to perform well.

Don't give employees make-work assignments. Don't make them go to unnecessary meetings. Don't even make them read unnecessary words in a memo.

Don't fill their time for them. Show them what needs to be done. Show them how to do it. Make sure they have the tools they need. Then get out of the way and let them do it. When you tell them, by what you do, that you trust them to do things right, they'll be motivated to do that.

SECOND PRINCIPLE OF TIME MANAGEMENT FOR MOTIVATION

Make sure the time savers are really saving time.

I recently visited a large Wisconsin company to do some on-site time management training. As the VP in charge of training led me through the maze of cubicles to the classroom, I noticed a couple of folks standing by the fax machine. As the machine started to whir, one reached out and tugged on the sheet of paper as it came out of the machine. Faxing was no longer fast enough.

We use the fax to speed up communication, right? But then we start faxing stuff that could just as well go by surface mail, and we wait until the last minute to write that letter so that it has to go by fax.

Somebody has to spend time selecting the fax, servicing the fax, maintaining the fax, and replacing the fax with a new, improved, faster fax with voice mail—bought with the capital somebody had to work to produce.

How much have we really saved—in energy, money, and time? What happened to all that time the computer was supposed to save us? It probably got gobbled up in endless e-mail and "surfing the Net."

Don't get me wrong. I wouldn't want to go back to life before the computer, and I've even come to see the value of voice mail. But these good slaves can become horrible masters, driving us with their bells and beeps and buzzers, making it easier for the world to interrupt us and distract us. We wind up attending to everybody's business but our own. And we wind up with another job-related frustration—doing work but not getting the job done. That leads to an undermining of motivation.

THIRD PRINCIPLE OF TIME MANAGEMENT FOR MOTIVATION

Separate the important from the merely urgent.

List the three most important elements in your life. Now list how much time you spend on them in an average week. This can be a very painful exercise.

If you're like a lot of us, you wind up spending little time on the stuff that really counts—family and friends, spiritual growth, physical conditioning.

In the workplace, we somehow never get around to long-range planning or staff training, although we spend huge chunks of time each week responding to the clamor of the telephone, the e-mail, the fax, and other urgencies—usually dealing with problems that might have been prevented in the first place with better planning.

We end up exhausted and empty. We've worked hard, but we've made little or no progress on the things that really matter. We can't see the forest for the brush fires. We spend too much time fighting fires and not nearly enough time preventing them so they don't get in the way of really productive work.

 Take Care of the Important Stuff   Urgencies demand immediate attention. The important stuff can always wait—and so it always waits. Ironically, urgencies usually happen because you haven't attended to the important stuff.

The problems won't just go away—you have to make them go away. You won't "find" time to work on long-range goals. You have to make time. And if you make the effort to do that for yourself and others, it affects motivation in a positive way because you and your employees know you are concentrating on the right activities, not fixing problems that probably shouldn't have occurred.

 Make Time   Set aside time each week for the thinking and reading, meeting and talking that never seems to get done. Mark this time on your calendar, and keep that appointment, just as you'd keep an appointment with your boss or your most important client. And give your employees some time to do that as well. It will be the best time you spend on the job.

FOURTH PRINCIPLE OF TIME MANAGEMENT FOR MOTIVATION

Ask "why?" first.

You reach for your day planner like a gunfighter going for his pistol.

"We need to have a meeting."

"How's Monday at 9?"

"No good. I've got my marketing meeting."

"How about 10:30?"

"Nope. Weekly staff review."

"Lunch? Wait a minute. I've got a business lunch. How about...?"

And on it goes, until you either squeeze meeting time into an already overcrowded day or extend that work day, cutting time out of real life.

Let's start over.

"We need to have a meeting."

Steady now. Don't go for that calendar.

Ask "Why?" That is the magic question.

However you say it, say it! You may find that you're able to solve the problem with a minute's worth of conversation right now. You may be able to clarify the situation until you discover there's really no problem. You may determine that you're not the right person to handle the problem.

After "Why?" ask "Why now?" for the phone calls and memos and faxes that demand your immediate attention. Some need doing right away. Some can wait. Some don't need your attention at all.

Ask "Why?" and "Why now?" and encourage the people who work with you to do the same. What will happen? They'll start focusing more on important activities that make a difference rather than on activities that merely take up time. And when people are making a difference and they know it, they feel more motivated to perform.

Fifth Principle of Time Management for Motivation

Leave holes in the calendar.

Once you start filling the slots, it's hard to stop. Out comes that calendar, again and again, until you've extended the workday beyond all reason and filled every available moment with activity.

Then and only then do you feel justified in saying "no." But by then it's too late. You have no time for your own agenda, no time to plan, no time to think, no time to figure out how to prevent problems and make things work better. Make time for doing these things, and you will have time for everything else.

Reading the Symptoms   Count on it. Some activity will *always* take longer than you planned. And there's *always* an emergency. But taking longer and always confronting emergencies are really symptoms of poorly managed time and poorly managed processes.

Keep Some Free Time   Leave holes in the calendar for planning and figuring out how to improve. Encourage the people you work with to do the same. We always feel more motivated to do things right than to fix things that go wrong.

SIXTH PRINCIPLE OF TIME MANAGEMENT FOR MOTIVATION

Allow enough time for the task.

It's 1:26 now. If the traffic is light and you hit the signals, you should be able to get to your next call in, oh, 14 minutes. The call should take, say, 20 minutes, and then 14 to get back, so you can schedule your conference call for precisely 2:14.

And you can be pretty damn sure you won't be back in time to take it. Traffic won't be light. You'll miss a signal. Your appointment will keep you waiting.

 Get Real   Be realistic in your planning. Don't overstuff the schedule. And yes, encourage the people who work with you to do the same. This way you'll get what's important done and reduce the frustration (and compromised motivation) that comes from rush, rush, rush, and not quite getting things done.

And one thing more—take along something you want or need to do while that next appointment keeps you waiting.

SEVENTH PRINCIPLE OF TIME MANAGEMENT FOR MOTIVATION

Relearn how to do one thing at a time.

Watch a kid at play. Have you ever seen such concentration? That kid really doesn't hear Mom calling to come in for supper. He's in another world, the world of his own mind.

Now watch this kid all grown up and at work. He's on the phone, jotting notes, eyeing the computer screen, and eating a sandwich—and paying attention to none of it.

Getting a lot done? Probably not. Probably not getting much of anything done, really.

What should you do instead? Practice doing one thing at a time, and encourage your coworkers to do the same. When you're having a conversation, concentrate on that conversation rather than thinking about your next project or appointment. Give people and tasks your total, undivided attention. You and your coworkers will be amazed at how much you'll accomplish. You'll get done faster and do the job better, with little need for clarifying or revising or fixing later. And you'll notice that you and others will naturally feel more motivated because you're getting good results.

WHAT DO YOU DO WITH ALL THE TIME YOU SAVE?

And what are you going to do with the time you and your coworkers start saving with all this time management? You could always find more that needs doing, of course. But before you spend all your time, consider this: There's no greater reward you can give yourself and your colleagues than a little time off.

In this lesson you learned seven tips for how to better manage time, get more important things done, and feel more motivated.

12

REDUCING STRESS AND ENHANCING MOTIVATION

In this lesson you'll learn how to help employees reduce the stress that gets in the way of performance and undermines motivation.

STRESS AND PERFORMANCE

A researcher named Hans Selye told us all about stress many years ago. It's time we started listening to him.

Selye studied the physical and mental effects of long-term stress. He was the first to use the term "stress" in the sense we use it today when we talk about being "under a lot of stress" or "stressed out," a state usually about a step-and-a-half away from "burnout." While a little bit of stress may be helpful and is perfectly natural, high stress is a symptom of poor management and ultimately undermines motivation.

 Stress   A physical and psychological reaction to challenge, danger, and change in the environment.

Stress isn't "out there" in the world (although sources of stress certainly are). Stress is inside us, the emotional and psychological responses to life's stressors. Too much stress, endured for too long a time, can hurt us, open us up to serious illness, and ultimately even kill us.

Stressors are everywhere; stress is unavoidable. Bad stuff is stressful, but so is good stuff.

- Getting evicted from your apartment is stressful—and so moving into your dream house.

- Getting fired is stressful—and so is getting a new job.

- Breaking up is hard to do—but so it getting married.

- Working too hard is stressful, as most of us know only too well—but so is going on vacation.

A vacation stressful? Sure, if you think about it. Your routine is disrupted. You don't have any of the familiar pleasures and comforts that help ease you through the day. When you wake up in the darkness, you aren't even sure which way to go to find the bathroom. You take on new roles—travel agent, long-haul driver, and recreation director—roles you may or may not feel competent to tackle.

And what about Christmas? A nightmare of stress for many, made worse by the fact that the whole world is relentlessly telling us how happy we're supposed to be.

But it doesn't take Santas on every corner and *It's a Wonderful Life* on every TV station to stress us. Daily life—with its traffic and noise and confusion—is plenty stressful enough. Some days we're ready for a rest before we even show up for work in the morning.

WHY LACK OF STRESS ISN'T THE ANSWER TO THE STRESS PROBLEM

So as a leader of your coworkers it's your job to help everybody chill out by removing all stress in the workplace, right?

You couldn't even if you tried, and even if you could, you wouldn't want to. A total lack of stress is not only impossible but also undesirable.

To illustrate the point, consider the plight of a colleague of mine who retired a few years ago. Oh, how he looked forward to that happy day. He planned to fill his days reading and puttering in perfect contentment. But when I ran into him a few weeks after his retirement party, he didn't look like the happy, carefree guy I expected. "I don't know what to do with myself," he confided to me. "I got all caught up on my reading and puttering after about two days."

All puttered out and no place to go. No reason to get up in the morning, nothing to shower and shave for, no one expecting him or relying on him, no problems to solve, no paycheck to validate his sense of self-worth. In short, nothing to tell him that his life has meaning and purpose.

Too much stress is harmful, but not enough isn't good, either. We're really aiming for "eustress," a term Selye coined to indicate the ideal level of stress in each life.

 Eustress   The state of life when it's not too hot and not too cold but juuuuust right.

Where is that ideal level? It's different for each of us. Just as we all have different thresholds of pain, different tolerances for boredom, different abilities to handle chaos, and different energy levels, we all have different tolerances for and abilities to handle stress.

Just to make it a little tougher to figure, one worker's stressor is another's challenge is a third's lark. Some folks enjoy "working a room," pumping hands and exchanging small talk, for example. For others, such activity is torture almost beyond enduring, while others just find the drill boring.

 All You Can Do Is Help   So, how can you possibly create eustress for your coworkers? You don't. You help and encourage them to find it for themselves. This is a state in which their motivation is high and their frustration is low—and their stress level is just right.

We're not talking about encouraging goofing off here. We're talking about healthy self-maintenance.

 Monitor and Control Stress   Create a working environment in which workers can monitor and control stress, thus maintaining peak performance.

Helping workers manage time productively will help, of course, as will matching the worker with his or her right work, as we've seen in previous lessons. But you can go a step further by encouraging your coworkers to go on mini-vacations and fitness breaks.

STOP HER! SHE'S ON A ROLL!

Getting started is often the toughest part of any task. (Thus the adage, "Well begun is half done.") Once you're over that initial resistance, and once you establish a productive rhythm for the work, you hate to stop. You want your momentum to carry you along.

Coffee keeps your caffeine level high, and that doughnut supplies a sugar high, allowing you to keep working right past fatigue. That surge of adrenaline as the deadline draws close gives you the heady feeling that you're really flying. Then comes the crash.

Just as revving a car engine too fast for too long can damage the engine, running your own engine too fast can eventually damage your system. We all know that. But here's the surprise. It can also keep you and your coworkers from working as efficiently and effectively as might be possible. And this will chip away at people's motivation to do their jobs, because too much is going on and the results don't seem commensurate with the efforts.

 Better Under Pressure? Not! You really don't work better under pressure. When you work beyond your comfortable endurance level, coordination and mental agility both dip. You start making mistakes, and you stop having ideas.

THE PLIGHT OF THE ADRENALINE JUNKIE

The story gets worse. Stress is cumulative. The longer you keep that engine revved up, maintaining an unsafe level of stress, the harder it becomes to relax when the job is finally done. You can wind up at the end of the day exhausted but unable to sit still, let alone sleep. You can't enjoy food, conversation, or leisure, and you don't get your proper rest. You start the next work cycle still tired and drawn from the last one.

Some organizations have gone to great lengths to help employees break this stress cycle. Recognizing the therapeutic value of exercise in reducing stress, for example, Land's End, the direct-mail marketers, built their employees a multi-million dollar exercise facility for workouts and recreation.

That's not likely to happen at most workplaces. But there are lots of cheaper and easier ways to help your coworkers break the stress cycle—and keep their motivation high.

TAKING A VACATION—SEVERAL TIMES A DAY

Encourage your colleagues to take several mini-vacations each day—not when the work is done, but when the stress is building. Then set a good example by practicing what you preach.

FOUR MINI-VACATIONS THAT DON'T COST A PENNY

Here are four ideas for taking brief on-the-job vacations.

1. *Deep breathing.*

When you get stressed, you stop breathing, or breathing properly, at least. Your breathing moves from low in the gut up into the throat. You draw in ever-smaller gulps of life-sustaining oxygen.

Nervousness will do the same thing to you, which explains why your voice may become high and squeaky when you make a presentation in front of a group.

The shallow breathing that stress provokes isn't as obvious as the gasping of the terrified public speaker. Often you probably aren't even aware that your breathing has shifted. But if it goes on long enough, you'll become light-headed, fatigued, even disoriented.

The solution: Take time out to breathe. Put your hands on your stomach and feel it rise as you draw air all the way down to the base of your spine. Let the air out slowly. Take another long, deep, cleansing breath and let it out. Do this several times, flooding your system with oxygen. A sense of relief and well-being washes over you. After a minute or two, you're relaxed and rested and ready to return to the task with renewed energy and enthusiasm.

2. *Day tripping.*

Think of a place where you were contented and relaxed. Maybe it's a favorite vacation spot. See yourself as you were there, perhaps sitting on the bank of a mountain lake, fishing pole in hand, mind on idle, waiting for a bite but not really caring whether you get one, almost hoping you don't, so perfect is your sense of contentment.

But you're a long way from that quiet lake, and it's a long time until your next vacation. Go there right now. Take a two-minute mini-vacation by closing your eyes and imagining the scene as clearly as you can. Just experience it.

3. *Deep space zero.*

Teachers don't like it when students daydream in the classroom, and bosses don't like it when employees do it in the workplace. We figure it's a waste of time.

But daydreaming is natural, healthy, and relaxing. (It can also result in some pretty spectacular ideas, but we're not worrying about practical outcomes right now.) Build a little legalized daydreaming into the daily routine. Spend a few minutes letting your mind wander. Since I've learned to think with my fingers, I often do my daydreaming by typing out whatever I'm thinking, free-associating by letting my thoughts lead me instead of the other way around. But you need only close your eyes and relax those mental reins for a bit.

Bosses Cause Stress   It's useful to remember that a boss—a person who always wants to tell others what to do—is a major cause of stress on the job and of why people lose their motivation to perform. Don't be a boss—be a coach and helper.

4. *Body tuck and jive.*

Lots of folks feel their stress in the gut, suffering from stomach pains and cramps by the end of a long, stressful day. Others come home from work with a stress headache or a stiff, sore neck that keeps them miserable all night.

We take our stress out on our bodies. When I'm tense, I clench my jaw and tense my shoulders—without even knowing I'm doing it. I wind up at the end of the day with sore shoulders, a jaw that aches so much I can barely chew my dinner, and no idea where the pain came from. Where do you feel your stress?

The trick is to catch yourself tensing or grinding before you develop a literal pain in the neck or head or butt or wherever. Then take a body break. I massage the joint where my upper and lower jaws meet. I let my shoulders drop and relax, gently rotating them as I feel pain and tension drop away.

You don't need a degree in physical therapy, and you don't need a lot of time. You just need to remember to do it.

A Hard Habit to Break   You won't remember to take a break—not at first, anyway. Habits are very hard to break, and routines take on the force of natural law. You may need to post a relaxer-reminder on the computer screen, the coffee pot, the drill press, wherever you'll see it at the right time.

Talk this over with your coworkers. Encourage them to take four or five short (two- to five-minute) breaks a day. Reinforce each other with friendly reminders to breathe, to dream, to drop the shoulders.

Don't Wait Too Long   Don't wait until you've finished a project to take your stress break. If the project drags on, it may drag you too deeply into the stress cycle. And if you take a break right in the midst of a project, you'll be able to return to it and start right in again, without any warm-up time.

THREE MORE WAYS YOU CAN HELP YOUR COWORKERS GET UNSTRESSED

1. *Create a quiet place.*

A room or space or corner where folks can sit and put their feet up and sip coffee or chat or read or eat lunch or do nothing works wonders.

2. *Create a quiet time.*

Arrange schedules so that each coworker can have some time each day without interruptions—no phones, no meetings, no taps on the door.

And then remove the biggest stressor of all.

3. *Link authority with responsibility.*

What would you expect to find on a list of the most stressful jobs in America? Cop? Firefighter? Air traffic controller? They're there, all right, along with roofer, urban bus driver, and other occupations obviously requiring iron guts, steel nerves, and the mental makeup of a tightrope walker.

But some of the others on the hit list might surprise you—jobs such as clerk, secretary, and middle manager. And a few other occupations might surprise you by their absence—jobs such as president and CEO, positions at the top of the heap often associated with the need to make tough decisions in a hurry.

Secretary more stressful than CEO? What gives?

The CEO has a great deal of responsibility. But he or she also has the authority to deal with those responsibilities and the power to make decisions that matter.

The secretary also has a great deal of responsibility—not of the same kind or perhaps even the same size as the CEO's, but a lot of responsibility nonetheless. What he or she often lacks is the power to make meaningful decisions.

Needed: Authority Responsibility without authority is a sure formula for stress in the workplace. When people are charged with getting certain things done but have to check in with someone else to make necessary decisions, the result is stress, the kind that gets in the way of motivation.

Delegate Authority Give your coworkers the authority they need to meet their responsibilities. If you tell your administrative assistant to make sure all the time sheets are filled out properly and filed on time, for example, also give her the authority to impose the appropriate standards and deadlines—and make sure everybody knows you've done so. If you don't, you've set her up for failure—and stress.

The health and well-being of your coworkers is more important than any work goal you can name. It's also good business and smart management. Rested, unstressed employees work more efficiently and effectively—and are motivated to perform better.

In this lesson you learned how to help employees reduce the stress that gets in the way of performance and undermines motivation.

13

Don't Just Train the Worker—Educate the Person

In this lesson, you'll learn how to use training and education as another way to enhance motivation and performance.

If you want them to do the job right, you have to give your work force the proper tools. One of those tools is education.

Some training needs are obvious. If you introduce a new computer system into the workplace, you have to train your workers to use it. It isn't fair to expect them to "just pick it up" or learn the system on their own time.

Are you overlooking other, less obvious training needs? Survey your coworkers. Do they need skills training and updates—or has your organization simply expected them to "keep current" or "adapt" on their own?

tip

Go to Bat for Your People   If you can't authorize the training your workers need yourself, become the advocate for your team, persuading upper management by arguing through common goals: "To get the productivity we want, we must give them the training they need."

Support training efforts by making sure workers are covered when they're off-site receiving that training and that their job evaluations reflect the learning and growth they've achieved.

Do all that, and the training still might backfire. If not presented properly, training can become a punishment instead of a perk.

Case in point: Patty wasn't happy, and neither was her manager. "Why do I have to take the time-management workshop?" Patty grumbled to fellow members of the secretarial pool. "Don't they think I manage my time well?"

"You talk about bad attitude," her manager muttered to another unit administrator. "I give her a day off with pay to get some training, and she pulls a long face and barely speaks to me the rest of the week."

The manager saw the training as a way to help this worker. The worker saw it as a not-so-subtle indication that she wasn't performing well.

Training as a Chance to Get Better, Not as an Indicator of Poor Performance

So why did giving Patty the opportunity to get some training come across as looking like she wasn't performing well?

- She didn't have a choice. She was ordered to attend.
- She didn't feel that she needed the training.
- She saw the training as an indication of management's low opinion of her abilities.

From that perspective, will Patty be motivated to take the training seriously or use what she learns to perform better? Not likely.

So what's a better way to go about this?

- Present training opportunities as indications that you are happy with performance and want the person to learn even more.

- Offer a range of relevant training choices.

- Explain the choices in terms of what they'll do for the worker.

- Speak to specific worker needs and benefits of training to that worker.

Do these things, and you have the right to expect reasonable return on your investment of money and worker time. Hold that worker accountable for reporting back on the substance of the training and its applications to the workplace.

And one thing more—don't hesitate to attend the training with them, as an equal, if you can also benefit from the instruction. That way you send the message that *"we'll* benefit from this" rather than *"you* need this." And it will also help you keep up with them!

FINDING THE RIGHT TRAINING

The more training options you can develop, the better choices you'll be able to make. This will allow you to make sure your employees keep growing in their skills, making them more able to perform well, which feeds their motivation to perform because they know they are doing well. And that feels good. Here are some options to consider.

PRO TRAINERS

Get on the mailing list for Career Track, Fred Pryor, American Management Association, and other for-profit trainers. You'll have to wade through a lot of material that won't be relevant to you, but you might also discover the right offering at the right time at the right price.

Your Local Community College and/or University

Send for the catalog from your nearest university or college extension or outreach. They offer everything from low-cost, hands-on computer training to stress management and conflict resolution in the workplace. You'll find a wealth of options for yourself as well as your workers.

These programs are usually short duration—one night per week for a few weeks or even a complete program in a single day.

Some of these programs may offer college credit, and the non-credit offerings usually carry some sort of continuing education unit or similar certification. Many adult education institutions, especially in areas such as business, organizational communication, and library science, often offer certificate programs as well.

Your organization can increase the value of these programs for your coworkers by building step raises for credits into the compensation package.

Trade and Tech Schools

Get the schedule for the local technical or vocational school. Classes are low-cost and give your coworkers a chance to develop and refine skills. Again, some may carry transferable college credits, and you can reward the learner with credit on the salary schedule.

Don't Overlook Special Training Needs and Opportunities

A computer programmer needs computer programming. A data processor needs data processing. Anybody who works with machinery needs to keep current on their equipment. Folks need updates on relevant government regulations in their areas of concern.

Sometimes the need may not be so overt but may be every bit as important. The sheriff in Dane County, Wisconsin, hired me to take every officer in his department through a full-day training on "how to be interviewed by the media," complete with live sessions in front of a camera. He expected each officer to function as a spokesperson for the department if the situation called for it, and he wanted to make sure they were prepared to meet his expectation.

The machinist might want and need to be on at least speaking terms with the computer, and everyone, from the receptionist to the CEO, might benefit from training on stress management.

Let the Trainee Become the Trainer

If you really want to learn something well, just try explaining it to someone else. Everybody wins when the trainee becomes the trainer. Send a coworker to a training, then ask her to share what she learned with a small group back in the workplace.

 Keep Your Eyes Open   Look for opportunities to expand training into education.

SOMETIMES TRAINING BECOMES SOMETHING MORE—AN EDUCATION

It's a matter of approach more than subject matter. What you want is for employees to internalize what they learn, take ownership of it, and want to use it to perform better. What I'm talking about here isn't just training, but education:

- Training is passive; the learner receives. Education is active; the learner creates.

- Training requires memorizing information. Education requires application of the information to life situations.

- Training provides answers. Education develops questions.

- Training focuses on facts and methods. Education centers on understanding and performance.

- Training prizes unchanging facts and answers. Education rewards a flexible approach to problem-solving.

- Training is short-term and limited. Education is forever.

- We train workers. We educate whole people.

And this reminds us of Henry Ford's lament: "Why is it that I always get a whole human being when all I want is a pair of hands?" The fact is that what we really want is not a pair of hands, but whole persons using all their abilities to perform well if we want to compete today. This means creating an environment in which they feel motivated to perform. And it means supporting them with the training and education they need to take full advantage of their abilities.

BASIC TRAINING: SHARING THE BIG PICTURE

No matter what other kind of training you offer the people who work with you, there's one kind of educational opportunity every leader should provide—fundamental knowledge of the operation of the organization.

That means awareness of the big picture—long-term goals and objectives. It means reasons for specific projects and parts of projects. It also means access to the numbers—exactly where the organization stands financially.

 Spoon-Feed It to Them   It isn't enough to keep this sort of operating information in a book in an office, technically available but for practical purposes invisible. You should provide the information, whether your coworkers ask for it or not. Remember, they can't identify with the organization if they don't know much about it.

When you share information openly and actively, you'll earn their trust and exhibit your trust in them. You'll also help your coworkers develop as partners, capable of participating in decision-making and problem-solving.

In this lesson, you learned how to use training and education as another way to enhance motivation and performance.

IF YOU WANT TO KEEP THEM MOTIVATED, YOU'VE GOT TO EARN THEIR TRUST

In this lesson you'll learn what you must do—and what you must never do—to earn and keep employees' trust.

TRUST, LEADERSHIP, AND MOTIVATION

You can be a master of many of the management and leadership skills I've reviewed in this book. But none of these things will help one bit if the employees don't trust the manager (the subject of this lesson) and the manager doesn't trust the employees (the subject of the next lesson).

They don't have to like the manager (although life is surely a lot nicer for everybody if they do). The manager has to make the tough calls and enforce the unpopular edicts from upper management. So, not everything the manager does will be gladly accepted. But that's part of the job.

Leadership is not a popularity contest. It's also not necessarily about being entertaining or dynamic or charismatic. Employees don't have to think the manager is smarter than they are. They don't even have to think about the manager much at all.

But they have to trust their manager, or this individual can't lead them. Further, employees will have little motivation to work with a manager they do not trust.

If you're a new manager, folks will be understandably skeptical, especially if you're trying to walk right into a leadership role from the outside. "Just who are you," they may be thinking, "to come in here and tell me what to do?"

Even if you've come up through the ranks and worked with them for years, they might be suspicious of you in your new role, watching you closely to see if you "go management" on them. You may be guilty until proven innocent.

 Earn It Don't demand or ask for trust. Just begin acting in a trustworthy fashion, from day one, all day, every day. This means employees can depend on you to help when help is needed and get out of the way when employees need some independence.

Trust builds slowly, over days and weeks and months. By consistently supporting people, coaching them when needed, and giving them the authority and responsibility they need to perform, the trust will come.

THE TRUTH, THE SAME TRUTH, AND NOTHING BUT THE TRUTH

One way trust comes to a manager is through always telling the truth, whether it's good or bad. If a person gets caught in a lie even once, people will have hard time ever believing that individual again. A hundred truths can't wipe out that single lie.

People lie for many reasons, but the reasons often fall into one of two categories:

- People lie to avoid hurt feelings.
- People lie to save face.

Whatever the reason, the lie will always come back to haunt a person. Trust and truth are intimately related. And if you are consistently truthful with employees, you can expect that in return. There will be a shared view of situations, an important component of why an employee will feel motivated or not.

Tell It Straight   Make sure your "yes" means "yes" and your "no" means "no." Don't say "yes" because it's what they want to hear. Don't downplay a problem or poor performance, even though you know they don't want to hear what you must say. Firm but considerate criticism that focuses on the behavior and not the person will generate trust and reinforce motivation.

Top Secret   You may not be able to tell the *whole* truth. As a manager, you may at times be asked to carry the organization's secrets. But even in withholding information you must be absolutely truthful.

Never say "I don't know" if you know. Never say "I don't have that information" if you have it. Never say "I'll tell you later" if you have no intention of telling them later. Instead, tell them why you can't tell them.

"We'll see" is a lie if you have no intention of re-evaluating your decision. "I'll get back to you on that" is a lie if you have the answer now but just don't have the guts to reveal it—now or later.

It's fine to say "I don't know" when it's the truth, of course, but it's an incomplete answer. You need to follow it up with "I'll try to find out for you" or "I'll have that for you Friday morning" or "You should ask Sarah in personnel."

MATCH YOUR ACTIONS TO YOUR WORDS

If you say you'll do it, do it. If you say you'll be there, be there. If you find that you can't do what you said you'd do or show up when you said you'd show up, tell your coworkers, and tell them why.

Workers have special disdain for the leader who turns out to be "all show and no go." Don't promise what you can't deliver. On the other hand, there is nothing more powerful to engender trust than for a person to do what he says he will do. Of course, this also suggests that what a manager does will foster cooperation and competence.

Walk the Walk   If you don't walk your talk, you'll find yourself walking alone. Nobody follows a leader they don't trust.

FOUR REASONS WHY WE DON'T TELL THEM ENOUGH

Yes, you'll have to withhold information at times. But a lot of managers hold back a lot more than they need to. They do it because:

- They think they're supposed to.

- That's how their managers treated them.

- It's always been done that way.

- Knowledge is power, and they're reluctant to give up power.

None of these are good reasons. Share information with employees as freely as possible, especially as that information directly affects your coworkers' status or well-being on the job. That includes the numbers—the financial status of the organization—and an explanation of what the numbers mean.

The Whole Truth   If you flood employees with numbers, the numbers can be a kind of lie, too. This is because instead of revealing truth, they hide it. You need to convey information *and* the background and context they need to be able to understand that information. In that way, you invite trust and you create the sense of inclusion that contributes to employees feeling motivated.

INVITE AND PAY ATTENTION TO DISAGREEMENT AND CRITICISM

Nobody likes to be told he or she is wrong. But good leaders need to hear just that from the people they expect to lead.

Be prepared to provide reasons for your decisions, but also be ready to listen to your employees' arguments when they don't buy your reasons.

This is more than a matter of good manners and effective human relations. You'll learn something that helps you to be a better manager.

Don't tell them you'll think things over and then do things exactly the way you planned in the first place. If you intend to reaffirm your original decision, tell them so. At least they'll know they've been heard.

Don't coerce them or finesse them, recruit them or seduce them. *Level* with them.

Be Open to Dissenting Opinions   You'll never lose anything by listening to ideas contrary to your own. You can always affirm your original decision and the reasons for it. But you might gain information you need to make a better decision—along with the trust and respect of your coworkers.

DON'T GET CAUGHT IN A TRIANGLE

Triangles mean trouble—in work as well as in romance.

John comes to you with a complaint about Jean. You go talk about it with Jean. Then you go back and tell John what Jean said and what you think about what Jean said. You figure you've got things pretty well ironed out, but when you show up for work the next day, Jean's waiting for you with a list of grievances against John. So you go looking for John...

What's wrong with this picture?

You and John talk. You and Jean talk. You and John talk. You and Jean talk. Nothing gets settled, and John and Jean both end up figuring you for an untrustworthy so-and-so.

Let's back up and start over.

 Let's Have a Get-Together   When John comes to you with the problem about Jean, you need to get Jean into the picture. You, John, and Jean should do your talking together, so everybody hears the same thing at the same time.

After you're sure you understand both sides of the problem, you have a choice. Either send John and Jean away to figure out a solution themselves (often the best strategy) or make your decision, one decision, one time, and give John and Jean the news at the same time.

You may not please everybody, but you'll deal honestly with everybody, and you'll earn their trust.

ADMIT YOUR MISTAKES

They know you're human. They just want to make sure *you* know it.

You're going to make mistakes. Everybody does. The more pressure you're under, the more decisions you have to make in a hurry, and the more complex the problem, the more likely you are to make a mistake.

 Accept It and Move On   When you do screw up, take the hit. Accept responsibility, admit your mistake, and do what you can to make it right. That includes apologizing when an apology is appropriate. If you do that, people will respect you, come to trust you, and feel motivated to work with you.

Here are the things you *never* do:

- Never make excuses.
- Never try to shift the blame.
- Never scapegoat an employee.
- Never cover up to avoid looking bad.

Learn from the experience and make improvements so it's unlikely to happen again. If managers do this, their actions will communicate that they honestly want to do things right and that they want to help others as well. And these are actions that reinforce an employee's motivation to work with managers.

In this lesson you learned what you must do—and what you must never do—to earn and keep employees' trust.

15

TRUST HAS TO GO BOTH WAYS

In this lesson you'll learn how to trust your coworkers, how to show that trust, and how trust contributes to employee motivation.

They've got to trust you. You've got to trust them. It has to go both ways.

Trust A belief and confidence in the basic honesty, ability, and reliability of others.

You Gotta Have It If you don't trust your coworkers, you will never be able to lead them. Never. And you cannot expect them to feel very motivated to perform well.

WHY YOU CAN'T LEAD THEM IF YOU DON'T TRUST THEM

If you don't trust your employees, they'll focus on not making mistakes rather than on doing an outstanding job. Think about the difference that makes in the way you do your job. At best you'll have a cautious, timid performer, too frightened to take any sort of chance for fear of making a mistake.

If you don't trust them, they'll be glancing over their shoulders while they work. That doesn't work too well, either. We all tend to make more progress when we're looking ahead—and focusing on the task at hand.

And the consequences of lack of trust get even worse.

Living Up to Expectations   Some managers believe that if you trust employees, they may get sneaky, seeing how little work and how much messing around they can get away with. But here's something to appreciate: If this happens, it won't even be the employees' fault. It's just human nature. People live up (or down) to expectations. Expect a slacker, you may create a slacker.

DON'T THEY HAVE TO EARN YOUR TRUST?

Employees absolutely do not have to win your trust. They have to "earn" your distrust. You (or somebody in your organization) hired them. That means (or should mean) that the organization believes they can do the job they were hired to do. It also means (or should mean) the organization is committed to provide necessary training, information, tools, and support for them to continue to be able to do the job, even if their job changes.

Let Them Succeed   A worker is innocent until proven guilty, competent until proven incompetent, able until proven unable. In other words, it's important, if you want people to maintain their motivation to perform, that you think the best of them and assume they can perform. Make sure you remove any roadblocks that get in the way of that (including negative management attitudes).

Demonstrate Your Trust   It isn't enough that you trust them. They have to *know* you trust them. In human relations, perception is reality. So demonstrate your trust by proactively giving employees the responsibility and authority to perform.

How will they know whether you trust them? Does this happen because you say, "I trust you"? You know better than that. By your actions will they know you.

A Way to Show You Trust Your Coworkers: Respect Their Privacy

Several years ago I taught a writing workshop in the newsroom of the Minneapolis *Star-Tribune*. I encountered a great deal of tension, which I attributed to justifiable resistance at the notion of having some out-of-state "expert" come in and tell experienced, highly skilled professionals how to do their jobs.

Turns out there was more to it than that—much more. Reporters were steaming because their editors were "spying" on them, monitoring their work on networked computer screens as they wrote.

I didn't blame them for being steamed. An editor, of course, has the right and responsibility to read, comment on, and tear up a reporter's work (although our friend Clarke Stallworth has already told us why ripping up someone's work isn't effective). But it's dishonest to peek at the work without the worker knowing it.

Some of the reporters did more than just get mad. Some created secret, masked computer files to hide their work until it was ready.

 No Need to Be Sneaky   No secret monitors. No one-way mirrors. No lapel tape recorders. Any checking up you feel you have to do must occur out in the open.

Just this week a supervisor had a question for me after a seminar on stress management, during which I had delivered my thoughts on giving coworkers frequent stress breaks.

"So, I should just let them play computer games?" he asked with a concerned frown.

"What's the problem with computer games?" I asked back. ("Expert" consultants almost always answer a question with a question. Have you noticed that?)

"They're playing them during work time."

"Ah. And that's a problem because...?"

The frown of concern deepened into a frown of confusion.

"They're not supposed to."

"How's their performance?" I pressed. "Are they getting their work done?"

"Well, yeah."

"And their work is up to snuff?"

"Yeah."

"Then you've got no problem."

 Performance Is What Counts Focus on performance. If the performance meets or exceeds the standards you've set, you have no complaint about how a worker rests in between productive periods.

I'm not saying you don't have the right to create a rule against playing computer games on the job. I am urging you to make sure you need such a rule—and that you're willing and able to enforce it, evenly and consistently—before you issue any such rule.

If folks are getting their work done and doing it well, and if you're really respecting those workers' privacy, you shouldn't even *know* they're playing computer games.

But you're the supervisor. Don't you have to know what they're doing every minute? Of course not. You need to know if they're getting their work done, and you need to help them do it well.

Respect What They Already Have   You aren't granting your coworkers the right to privacy. They come to work with that. You're simply recognizing and respecting the right they already have. Same with free speech and a lot of other rights we believe to be fundamental. If you seek to curtail these or any other rights, you'd better have a compelling reason to do so. And you had better recognize that this is going to negatively influence their enthusiasm and motivation.

ISSUE SPECIFIC REPRIMANDS, NOT GENERAL EDICTS

Suppose you've got a worker who plays computer solitaire, plays it a lot, right out in the open, where you can't help but notice. And suppose this worker isn't getting his work done on time—or at all.

Too often, management response is to issue a general edict to all workers, banning all playing of computer solitaire and every other computer game at any time on the job.

What happens? The good and faithful who have been performing well stop playing solitaire on their ten-minute breaks—and start grumbling about what a mean-spirited place they have to work in. The solitaire junkie goes underground, playing just as much solitaire, but keeping it a much better secret.

Management has gained nothing and lost a lot. The poor performer is still failing to perform, and good workers have been punished for something they didn't do. And some supervisor—perhaps you—gets saddled with the rotten job of playing computer cop to enforce the no-game rule.

No Generalizing   General edicts issued to discourage particular behavior will always generate resentment among workers and waste management time.

The problem isn't computer solitaire. The problem is poor performance. Deal with the specific problem of one worker's poor performance specifically and directly. Any other response is inappropriate and unfair.

When You Hand Out the Responsibility, Hand Out the Authority Along With It

I'm "just your secretary." Hear my lament. I know you make the rules, and I don't resent that. It's your job. But I'm the one who gets the complaints when somebody fouls up on the job site. And I'm the one who gets the questions when you aren't here to answer them. I can't blame folks for getting mad—but I sure don't like it that they get mad at me. And nothing gets settled when I have to tell them I'll take a message, so you can deal with it later. Please, please get me out of the middle.

The boss replies: Your job is to be in the middle, to screen calls, to handle as much as you can without having to bother me with it.

The solution: The boss needs to give the secretary as much authority as possible to handle those questions and complaints from the field. Then everybody wins.

We noted in an earlier lesson that giving a worker responsibility without authority creates stress. It also wastes a lot of work time while folks wait for the decision to be made.

And it also demonstrates a fundamental lack of trust. You want them to do the job? You've got to give them the tools. In this case, one of the tools is trust—the authority to carry out your rules within the guidelines you set.

 Let Them Do the Job Give them the information they need to communicate effectively with coworkers, clients, outside suppliers, and other agents. Then trust them to do it. The result is that they will take their responsibility seriously and will be motivated to do the right things.

In this lesson you learned how to trust your coworkers, how to show that trust, and how trust contributes to employee motivation.

16

How to Avoid Being the (Worst) Boss of the Year

In this lesson you'll learn from the actions of some of the worst "bosses" and how their actions destroy the motivation of employees.

You've learned a lot in a short time about being a manager and a leader who helps to release rather than restrict the motivation in employees. As you apply what you've learned, you'll become better and more confident on the job. But to reinforce this, let's read about some folks who aren't doing so well.

Learn From Mistakes We should always learn from our mistakes. We can learn from others' mistakes, too. Watch what others who lead do and the reactions they get.

Scrooge and Motivation

Remember Scrooge? He's the famous villain whose Christmas Eve conversion provides the good news in Charles Dickens' immortal *A Christmas Carol*.

Before receiving visits from the spirits of Christmas past, present, and to come, Scrooge was a real piece of work. He habitually overworks and underpays his poor, hapless book-keeper—his own nephew!—and begrudges even the day off he must allow for Christmas Day. "Bah! Humbug!" indeed.

Scrooge sees the error of his ways and becomes a generous, loving uncle and boss after the Christmas spirits reveal to him the suffering he causes others and his own fate—to be scorned and reviled in death, as he was in life. The people in Scrooge's life before he changed his behavior and attitude were moti-vated all right—motivated to disrespect and not listen to him, that is.

But this is not always so in real life, alas, where truth often outdoes even the evil fiction of Scrooge.

MEET REAL-LIFE, MODERN-DAY SCROOGES

A fellow named Jim Miller conducts a "Worst Boss of the Year" competition. Folks nominate their bosses and describe the disgusting and sometimes downright evil things their bosses do.

Miller never seems to lack for nominees. He gets tons of stories about bosses who:

- Ransack their employees' desks, waste baskets, and lockers

- Monitor phone calls and computer documents

- Believe it or not, hide in supply closets to try to over-hear workers' conversations

He hears about bosses who wait until a few minutes before quitting time to dump a large ASAP job on the worker's desk.

He gets complaints about bosses who demand unpaid over-time and others who just assume their workers will stay late and take extra work home nights and weekends.

Often, Miller reports, these are the same bosses who dock a worker for being two minutes late the next morning.

Miller collects tales of unfairly short lunch breaks, of rules against family pictures or other personalizing elements in the cubicle, of dress codes that would put a military school to shame. But the stories go well beyond that.

Drum Roll, Please, for the Worst Bosses of the Year—or Any Year

The owner of a pet store made an employee carry a 20-pound bag of cat litter up a steep flight of stairs. Not so bad, you say? The employee recently had open heart surgery, and the boss knew it.

You wouldn't treat a dog that way, would you? That boss provided the stress level conducive to heart problems, as did the boss who called the hospital to berate an employee about missing work. The worker was preparing to undergo major surgery.

How about the thrifty restaurant manager who picked through the garbage for bits of jelly and butter and uneaten rolls to "recycle" (by serving them to the employees)?

The 1995 winner of Miller's worst boss competition was a Mid-western sales manager who, at least according to the employee's report, ordered employees to return to work when they tried to help a coworker who had suffered a heart attack.

Fearing a drop in productivity, this same creep waited until the end of the business day to report that a missing employee had died.

The worker who submits the winning nominee to Miller's yearly competition gets a one-week, all-expenses paid trip for two to Hawaii. I figure that the winner doesn't take the boss along.

DOES *DILBERT* MAKE YOU LAUGH— OR WINCE?

Scott Adams is making a career out of chronicling the idiocies and indecencies of managers. Adams created *Dilbert*, a sadsack office worker trying to stay afloat in a sea of impossible deadlines, incomprehensible directives, and sadistic bosses. He has become the hero of cubicle dwellers everywhere, and *Dilbert* strips continue to crop up on bulletin boards and e-mail networks—often despite specific bans.

Adams relies on his fans to provide him with new material. No problem. He got so many good ideas about bad bosses, he has been able to quit his day job to devote his full time to *Dilbert*. He gets literally thousands of story ideas by e-mail each week.

Adams doesn't have to exaggerate much. Every time he shows management making yet another idiotic decision, folks by the thousands write to ask, "How did you know?" and "When did you work for my company?"

How about you? What's your favorite boss horror story, the worst thing a supervisor has ever done to you? Before you send it off to Jim Miller and Scott Adams, think about what your story and all these other tales from hell tell you about bad management and, thus, about good management. And think about how the behaviors these tales describe affected your motivation and that of others to do well—or not so well.

What Scrooge Can Teach Us

There are lessons about motivation from the experience of Scrooge and from the Dilberts of the world. Let's review some of those. First, let's list some basic tenets of bad management that come from the previous descriptions—behaviors you need to avoid unless you want a group of rebellious, unmotivated employees on your hands.

- In every case, the manager operates in complete disregard for the employees' well-being. Only the company's point of view was considered.

- In no case was a decision explained or put into a context that might have allowed the worker to see the reason for the request or order.

- In every case, the manager obviously assumed bad faith, dishonesty, or laziness on the part of the employee.

If You're In *Dilbert*, You're In Trouble   You don't just want to avoid winding up a winner in Miller's Bad Boss Sweepstakes or the subject of the next *Dilbert* strip. You want to do a lot better than that. You want your employees to feel motivated to regularly perform at peak levels. You want to enable them to make good decisions, solve problems, and function independently of your constant supervision.

So, turn Scrooge's negative lessons into positives by *always*:

- Acting with regard for your employees' well-being

- Explaining decisions and putting them in the larger context of overall goals

- Assuming the best about and expecting the best from your employees unless you are given reason to assume otherwise

Now relax. If you show up on any "Boss of the Year" list, it's going to be one for the best, not the worst. Why? Because your employees will be motivated to perform well, and when that happens, you're performing well, too.

In this lesson you learned from the actions of some of the worst "bosses" and how their actions destroyed the motivation of employees to perform well.

17

WHAT DO WORKERS *REALLY* WANT, ANYWAY?

In this lesson you'll learn the secret behind motivating employees to perform well—and it's the same thing that motivates you.

After about 10 years of "restructuring" and "downsizing," workers are understandably not very happy on the job.

We started this guide talking about what workers wanted on the job. Let's take another look.

THE WAY THINGS REALLY ARE

According to a recent survey reported in *Investor's Business Daily*, workers say their supervisors don't understand them and that they don't receive recognition or reward for good work.

Lots of top managers brag about their "participatory management" styles—stressing collaboration, information sharing, and communication. But the folks working for them say they haven't noticed the difference.

The Bureau of Labor Statistics reports that more than six percent of us now work a second job. That figure is probably low, because lots of folks don't report that second income to the IRS. A Gallup Poll puts the number at 16 percent.

The "extra" money goes to meet expenses and pay debts, leaving folks with no money *and* no time.

In a book called *The Overworked American*, Juliet Schor says that we're working 160 more hours a year than we did 20 years ago. That's like adding a thirteenth month of work to each year.

WHAT WE WANT FROM WORK

We may not be getting enough from work, but we want it all. When Gallup asked, folks said they wanted:

- More time for family, friends, and themselves
- Interesting work
- Financial security
- A chance to get ahead

Polls report that folks want good health insurance and other benefits more than anything (81 percent said "very important," outpolling any other factor). But "interesting work" tied with "job security" for second place at 78 percent.

Workers also put high value on the chance to learn new skills and to work independently. They want recognition and chances for promotion, and they want their work to matter— helping others and making a contribution to society.

They don't want stress, and they don't want to work nights or weekends.

None of this should surprise you. "They" are "you." Your workers want the same things you do.

It's Not About Money   If you figure folks are only in it for the money, you're missing the point—and the chance to get at what really motivates the people you work with.

AND WHAT YOU CAN DO ABOUT IT

You probably can't raise their pay. You don't determine the fringe benefits or the retirement plan. You can't keep from having to take work (or at least worry about work) home with you at night—much less prevent it from happening to them sometimes.

So what *can* you do? What's the single most important thing you can give workers (and yourself) on the job? A chance.

- Give them the chance to do good work and to be recognized for that work.

- Give them a chance to participate in making decisions that affect them.

- Give them a chance to solve their problems—and yours.

- Give them a chance to know exactly where they stand with you and with the company.

To give them that chance, you need to be more than a good manager. You need to be a leader. And you need to appreciate that, while you don't motivate employees, you're going to affect their motivation, either positively and negatively. Which will it be?

As their leader, you'll fight *for* rather than *with* your employees. It's a tough spot to be in: Upper management appointed you, but you really have to answer to the folks you're managing.

- You need to lead for commitment rather than manage for compliance.

- You need to have a vision of what you want the workplace to be, and you need to communicate that vision in clear, plain English.

- Then you need to give them lots of chances to talk back. Effective communication has to be a two-way street. Talk *with* them, not *at* them or *to* them.

- You need to earn their trust. You'll best earn that trust by talking truth and by living by your words.

- And you need to give them your trust—assuming the best about them until and unless they give you reason to think otherwise.

When things go well under your leadership, you need to let them take the bows for the work they've done. But when there's trouble, you need to stand up and take the brunt of it.

Despite my suggestion earlier that we might want to avoid the language of sports to describe the reality of the workplace, I yield the floor to legendary football coach Paul "Bear" Bryant, talking about why he gives the credit to his players:

- If anything goes bad, I did it.

- If anything goes semi-good, then we did it.

- If anything goes real good, you did it.

That attitude, Bryant reported, "builds a team with one heartbeat."

You've been getting these lessons in small bites, 10 minutes (or so) at a time. But I can sum it all up for you in one sentence. The sentence will probably sound familiar: Treat them the way you'd like to be treated. Or better yet, treat them like they'd like to be treated.

Yep. It's the good old Golden Rule. It's a fine guide for living a good life, to be sure. And it's also smart management. It works—because it works both ways.

They'll pick up behavior cues from you, remember, mirroring your behavior. Treat them with respect and get respect back. Treat them with disdain and disdain comes back at you (although masked perhaps, since, after all, you *are* the boss).

Assume the best; get the best.

Assume the worst—well, you get the idea.

Is it really that simple? Of course not.

 It Ain't Always Easy Nothing about dealing with human beings is simple. We're all complex and contradictory. Sometimes we don't know what we want, and sometimes we can't put it into words even when we do.

But the basic concept behind all good management practices really *is* that simple. Treat them the way you'd like to be treated. Don't forget what it felt like to be in their position.

Follow this concept, and you'll make good decisions, day by day, person by person. These will lead to actions and interactions that turn on rather than turn off the motivation that resides in all employees.

And you'll receive a kind of job satisfaction you've never before experienced, the satisfaction of knowing you did your
own job well—and you helped a lot of other people do theirs
well, too.

In this lesson you learned the secret behind motivating
employees to perform well—and it's the same thing that
motivates you. Keep this book handy for review. But more
important, go out now and "write" your own book on
leadership and motivation.

INDEX

A

accountability, 63, 73, 96
agendas, preparing, 32-33
authority
    coworkers, trusting, 115-116
    delegating, 93
    linking to responsibility, 92-93
automatic rewards, 53

B

bosses
    coaches, comparing, 59-60
    Dilbert, 120-121
    leaders, comparing, 9-11
    mistakes, avoiding, 117-120
    Scrooge, 117-118
    stress, 90
brainstorming
    employee problem-solving, 40-42
    ideas, encouraging, 40-42
    job responsibilities, defining, 44
breaks
    performance, 113
    stress, reducing, 91
busy work (time management), 76

C-D

calendars, *see* time management
clichés, 23
coaching, 10, 60-62
    accountability, 63
    bossing, comparing, 59-60
    control, 63
    criticism, 63
    Employees of the Month, 64
    example, 59-62
    goals, setting, 63
    lessons, 62-63
    rewards, 62
    winners, creating, 64-65
commitment, 12
    compliance, comparing, 12-14
    encouraging, 10
communication
    clarifying, 26-27
    passive, 25-26
    two-way (at meetings), 33
    see also language
compacts, 13-14
competition, 65
    competitive merit pay schedules, 64
    Employees of the Month, 64
compliance, 11
    commitment, comparing, 12-14
    excellence, comparing, 11

computers, evaluating as time
savers, 76-77
concentration (time
management), 81-82
consensus, seeking, 33-34
consultants, hiring, 39
contracts, comparing to
compacts, 13
control
    coaching, 63
    leadership, comparing, 12
cooperation, encouraging, 5
coworkers
    basic requirements, 4
    basic rights, 3
    cooperation, encouraging, 5
    criticism, 60
    decision-making, encourag-
      ing participation in, 5
    Golden Rule, 127
    rewards, 58
    rights, respecting, 114
    stress, reducing, 91-93
    teams, building, 126
    training, *see* training
    triangles, avoiding, 106-107
    trusting, 109-110
      demonstrating trust, 111
      expectations, 110
      leadership, 109-110
      respecting privacy,
        111-116
      responsibilities, 115-116
    wants, 3-4
    see also employees
criticism, 60
    inviting, 105-106
    private, 63

daydreaming (reducing stress),
89-93
deep breathing (reducing
stress), 88-93

Dilbert, 120-121
direction (visions), 16

E-F

edicts, comparing to
reprimands, 114-115
education, comparing to
training, 94, 99
effort, rewarding, 54
emergencies (time
management), 80
employees
    compacts (expectations), 14
    current situation, 123-124
    importance, 62
    job responsibilities,
      defining, 44
    mistakes, *see* mistakes
    needs, meeting, 8, 124-128
    problem-solving, 38-39
      brainstorming, 40-42
      exploring options, 40
    redirecting, 72
    responding, 39
    see also coworkers
Employees of the Month, 64
Employees of the Week, 57
environment
    positive, creating, 6
    stress, managing, 86
euphemisms, 26-27
eustress, 85
excellence, comparing to
excellence, 11
expectations, trusting
coworkers, 110
extinction, principle of, 47

faxes, evaluating as time
savers, 76-77
following up meetings, 36-37

G-K

Gallup Polls
    Americans working second
        jobs, 124
    worker desires, 124
generalizing, avoiding, 115
goals
    coaching, 10
    mistakes, correcting, 68
    setting, 63
Golden Rule, 127

habits, breaking, 91
honesty, *see* trust

ideas, brainstorming for, 40-42
information, withholding,
    104-105
insubordination, avoiding, 13

job responsibilities
    defining, 44
    positive reinforcement,
        48-50

L

language
    clarifying, 26-27
    clear, 25
    clichés, 23
    euphemisms, 26-27
    motivating, 20-21
    passivity, 25-26
    plain talk, 23-27
    understandable, 21
    word pictures, 20-23
leadership, 7-9
    accountability, 73
    bossing, comparing, 9-11
    commitment, encouraging,
        10
    compacts (expectations), 14
    control, comparing, 12

coworkers
    managing, 125-128
    trusting, 109-110
developing, 9
effectiveness, 70
management
    comparing, 8
    theories, 7
    management theories, 7
    popularity, 101
    responding to employees,
        39
    responsibilities, 9
    trust, 101-102
    truth, 104
    worker needs, meeting, 8,
        124-128
lying, 102-104

M-O

management theories, 7
managers
    leaders, comparing, 8
    mistakes, avoiding, 121-122
    responding to employees,
        39
    role, defining, 4
meetings
    agendas, preparing, 32-33
    communication, two-way,
        33
    consensus, seeking, 33-34
    effective, conducting, 30-37
    following up, 36-37
    ground rules, establishing,
        34-35
    motivating, 28
    preparing, 30-31
    records, 35-36
    regularly scheduled, 29
    value of, 28-30
mission statements,
    comparing to visions, 17

mistakes
  admitting, 107-108
  avoiding
    bosses, 118-120
    bossing, 117
    managers, 121-122
  correcting, 66-73
    don'ts, 68-73
    effectiveness, 70
    goals, 68
    helping employees, 70-73
    immediacy, 70
    *productive strategies,
      66-67*
    see also problem-solving
  learning from, 67
  responding to, 67-70
money (motivation), 125
motivation, 2
  compacts, 14
  directing, 2
  extinction, priciple of, 47
  language, 20
  management theories, 8
  meetings, 28
  mistakes, correcting, 66-73
  money, 125
  obediance, comparing, 11
  peak performance, 1-3
  positive reinforcement,
    45-51
    continuing, 47
    immediacy, 50-51
    job responsibilities, 48-50
    self-reinforcement, 48
  rewards, 52-54
    dangers, 53
    effective, 53-54
  sources, 2
  trust, 101-102
  undermining, 59

negativism, versus rewards, 57

obediance, comparing to
  motivation, 11

P-Q

participation, encouraging
  decision-making, 5
passive communication, 25-26
performance, peak
  breaks, 113
  encouraging, 4
  motivating, 1-3
  positive reinforcement, 51
  reviews, 51
  standards, communicating,
    2
  stress, 83-84
physical therapy (reducing
  stress), 90-93
pit bosses, see bosses
plain talk, 23-27
  euphemisms, 26-27
  passive communication,
    25-26
planning, realistic (time
  management), 81
policies, comparing to visions,
  18
positive reinforcement, 45-51
  continuing, 47
  extinction, principle of, 47
  immediacy, 50-51
  job responsibilities, 48-50
  performance reviews, 51
  rewards, comparing, 52
  self reinforcement, 48
positive environment,
  creating, 6
pressure, see stress
principle of extinction, 47
privacy, respecting (trusting
  coworkers), 111-116

problem-solving
    employees, 38-39
        brainstorming, 40-42
        exploring options, 40
    examples, 42-44
    mistakes, admitting,
        107-108
    questions, asking, 44
    reprimands, 114-115
    triangles, avoiding, 106-107
    see also mistakes, correcting
procedures, comparing to
    visions, 18
productivity (time
    management), 74-75
professional trainers, 96-97
promotions, 58

quality control, 63
questions, asking, 44, 78-79

R

recording meetings, 35-36
redirecting workers, 72
reinforcement, *see* positive
    reinforcement
reprimands, comparing to
    edicts, 114-115
requirements, basic coworker, 4
respect, encouraging peak
    performance, 4
responsibilities
    authority
        delegating, 93
        linking, 92-93
    coworkers, trusting, 115-116
reviews, *see* performance,
    reviews
rewards, 45, 52-54
    automatic, 53
    coaching, 62
    coworker familiarity, 55

dangers, 53
effective, 53-58
effort, 54
Employees of the Month, 64
Employees of the Week, 57
negativism, 57
peer, 58
positive reinforcement,
    comparing, 52
promotions, 58
tangible, 55-56
trophy, 56-58
winners, creating, 65
rights, respecting coworker, 3,
114
role, defining, 4

S

Scrooge (bosses), 117-118
self-reinforcement, 48
slogans, comparing to visions,
    18
spare time, managing, 82
stress
    bosses, 90
    effects, 87-88, 93
    eustress, 85
    habits, breaking, 91
    lack of, 85-86
    managing, 86
    performance, 83-84
    reducing, 91-93
        breaks, 91
        daydreaming, 89-93
        deep breathing, 88-93
        physical therapy, 90-91
        vacations, 88-91
    responsibilities, 92-93
    trusting coworkers, 115-116
subordinates, avoiding
    insubordination, 13
supervisors, *see* bosses

T-V

tangible rewards, 55-56
teams, building, 126
technical schools, 97
time management
    avoiding wasting time,
        75-76
    busy work, 76
    concentration, 81-82
    emergencies, 80
    free time, scheduling, 80
    planning, realistic, 81
    productivity, 74-75
    questions, asking, 78-79
    setting aside time, 78
    slowing down, 75
    spare time, managing, 82
    stress, managing, 86
    time savers, evaluating,
        76-77
    urgency, determing, 77-78
time motivation, 74
trade schools, 97
training
    accountability, 96
    attending, 96
    authorizing, 94
    basics, 100
    education, comparing, 94,
        99
    finding, 96-97
        professional trainers,
            96-97
        trade/technical schools, 97
    opportunities, recognizing,
        98
    organizational knowledge,
        100
    positive attitudes, creating,
        95-96
    trainees as trainers, 98
    troubleshooting, 95
trophy rewards, 56-58

trust
    actions, matching words, 104
    corporate secrets, 103
    coworkers, 109
        demonstrating, 111
        earning, 110
        expectations, 110
        respecting privacy,
            111-116
        responsibilities, 115-116
    criticism, inviting, 105-106
    earning, 102
    information, withholding,
        104-105
    leadership, 101-102, 104,
        109-110
    lying, 102-104
    mistakes, admitting, 107-108
    numbers, 105
    reprimands, 114-115
    triangles, avoiding, 106-107
two-way communication, 33

urgency, determing (time
    management), 77-78

vacations, reducing stress,
    88-91
visions, 15-19
    example, 18
    importance, 16-17
    mission statements,
        comparing, 17
    necessity, 16
    policies, comparing, 18
    recommendations, 19
    slogans, comparing, 18

W-Z

winners, creating, 64-65, 70-73
word pictures, 20-23
work rewards, 45
workers, see coworkers;
    employees